Doubles Wisdom
for
Every Level

Derek Myers

How to Gain Real Confidence on the Tennis Court

Thank you to my wife, Cheryl and my children,
Hannah and Caleb for your incredible love and support.

Thank you to the great tennis minds who shared with me their knowledge of this
sport. And, thank you to my students who trust me to pass on that knowledge.

Contents

INTRODUCTION

When tennis enthusiasts turn on their television to watch a match, typically they will see two professionals playing against each other, primarily from the baseline. These pros amaze fans as they display an incredible amount of speed, power, athleticism, and endurance. As impressive as these singles matches are, this type of tennis doesn't reflect the average American's experience on the tennis court. While there is a tremendous amount of attention placed on singles at the professional level, the average American adult tennis player plays doubles. Doubles requires strategic shot selection and positioning, precise execution, and a high degree of team chemistry. While generally less physically demanding than singles, doubles can be mentally challenging because there are four players on the court and additional angles available to both teams.

Whether you play singles or doubles, tennis is a great way to get physical and mental exercise and have fun in the process. Doubles makes it possible to think more creatively as there are so many options available to each player. The court is bigger, all four players have various strengths and weaknesses, and each player can either contribute to their partner's best tennis or their worst tennis (we'll get into team chemistry later in the book).

My desire to write this book comes from over 30 years of playing and coaching. I have had the privilege of seeing doubles played at the highest level by playing against top NCAA doubles teams from Stanford, Texas, Illinois, Duke, Notre Dame, etc., as well as ATP-level teams. I have also seen doubles at the lowest level, which is where every tennis player's journey begins. This book is a collection of experiences and observations I have made along the way. Some of the topics covered are not new, just explained in my words. Other topics are my own solutions, created to help myself as a player or to help others as their coach. The bottom line is that the subject matter in this book is covered in detail and is organized in a way to help maximize your results as a tennis player.

I have seen players make many different mistakes on the doubles court (shot selection, positioning, bad communication with their partner, etc.). Often, these mistakes aren't entirely their fault. To improve their games, they participate in clinics and get bombarded with catchphrases and shortsighted teaching and then wonder why they don't get any better. They may also practice stroke mechanics with the mindset that stroke improvement will take their game to another level. Most players do need improved stroke mechanics. But if strokes are the primary focus and the topics in this book receive little to no attention, then improvement will be severely limited.

Contrary to mistakes caused by others, there are many mistakes for which players can only blame themselves. They get comfortable hitting at certain targets or standing in particular areas of the court. A knowledgeable teaching pro might even tell them what they are doing wrong, but the player is not willing to change. Comfort zones can be dangerous on the tennis court, especially when it comes to doubles. As you read this book, examine yourself to discover your own comfort zones and determine how you're going to break free from them. Remind yourself that your ability to improve is directly related to your willingness to be uncomfortable.

In addition, give yourself time to practice and make mistakes. You're not going to read this book once, then go out in an important match and do it all correctly. The skills outlined in this book will take time to develop. Make sure you are diligent at practicing, but be patient in expecting results. Practicing can be done in a drill setting, preferably with four people on the court all trying to apply the principles listed in this book. Or, you can decide before certain matches that you are going to forget about winning and losing and play for the sake of improvement. Many times, a powerful desire to win is what prevents players from improving. Old habits quickly creep back in because it's more comfortable to play the "old way," and the comfort zone deceptively seems to provide the best chance to win.

As a word of encouragement, everything I have included in this book I have successfully applied to my own game. I have also taught these same skills to others who were also able to get results. For the doubles veterans, some of the topics covered will challenge your thinking and may require some reprogramming to achieve success. For the beginner, you have the advantage of programming these ideas without breaking bad habits because you are starting from scratch. Whichever category you fall under, you can be sure that to achieve success, you will need to practice. Again, I'm not talking about just forehands and backhands. This book goes beyond stroke improvement. It's about how to gain wisdom on the doubles court and become a well-rounded player.

I have two primary recommendations before we begin:

1. Study this book. Don't just read it. The more you study it, the quicker you will program your mind to remember the information. Tennis requires many physical and mental skills. It also requires that you perform these skills quickly. When the information becomes programmed mentally, it can then be executed in the small window of time available to you during a point. Before long, it will become second nature. Some of the topics we will cover can be complicated and detailed. However, if you analyze each topic carefully in a step-by-step process, you will see each one's importance and understand why I have included so much detail.

2. My second recommendation is that you strongly encourage your doubles partner(s) to also study this book. Many of the topics we will cover require that both partners are on the same page. Section 1 on team positioning and shot selection can essentially be thrown out if both partners aren't working together. Make sure you and your partner(s) study it and then go to work on the practice court so you are both in sync as often as possible.

It is important to note that the section on team positioning and shot selection includes drills for you to use in practice. In addition, it also includes what players NTRP (National Tennis Rating Program) 3.5 and below can expect, and what players NTRP 4.0 and above can expect. You might be asking, why is there a difference? Points played at a 3.0 level are very different from a 5.0 level. The fundamentals we will cover are true regardless of your playing level and must be mastered to see doubles improvement. However, there are certain patterns of play you can expect to see from most players within your playing level, which will require you to make in-match adjustments. The quicker you can identify a pattern and adjust, the quicker you can take control of that match. Let me explain it another way. In a chess match, when one player makes a move and says "Check," confidence is high because that player has made strategic moves and can see how they are going to win. In doubles, confidence grows when you see a pattern, adjust your formation and strategy, and then execute.

To obtain this high level of confidence, don't sell yourself short by only working on strokes. Learn the fundamentals outlined in this book and make sure you (and your partner) can execute them quickly. Then, you will be better able to not only read and anticipate your opponents' patterns, but also to adjust and proactively stay one step ahead…Check. Let's get started.

SECTION 1

TEAM POSITIONING
&
SHOT SELECTION

If you watch doubles matches regularly, you should pick up on the fact that there are many positioning strategies that can produce success. Advanced doubles players understand that where they stand on the court contributes to their success as much as where they hit the ball. The best doubles teams are also able to understand team positioning strategies and implement the appropriate one(s) depending upon their own strengths and weaknesses, as well as their opponents'.

One major problem many players have is that they don't have a proper starting point when it comes to positioning. When I say, "starting point," I am not referring to the start of a point. Most players know roughly where to be when the point starts, but they don't know where to be while the point is being played. By saying "starting point," I am referring to positioning fundamentals that must be understood and followed throughout an entire point. These fundamentals are the foundation upon which doubles wisdom can be built. Once they are mastered, in-match adjustments can be made when necessary based on patterns of play.

In my experience, many players try to adjust their positioning too often as individuals and not as a team. This causes confusion and results in open gaps that their opponents can exploit. These individual adjustments are sometimes made without the player even aware that it has occurred. Why would this happen? Comfort zones. Players tend to move based on where they like to be on the court. The longer the point goes on, the greater chance that one or more players will unknowingly gravitate toward a comfort zone and be out of position. As the match progresses, those same players try to adjust their shot selections to the way points are being played. But, they are doing so while standing in the wrong place on the court. Trying to make a good shot selection with perpetually bad court positioning will rarely produce success. This is why team positioning should be priority one on the doubles court.

It takes a high degree of concentration and teamwork to be aware of where you are at all times and execute proper positioning throughout an entire point. Still not sure if positioning is really that important? Look at it this way, if you and your partner are on the same page with your team positioning, then your shot selections should complement that positioning. In other words, your shot selections should be based on your positioning. Helping you understand how to be sure you and your partner are in the right position throughout a point is the positioning foundation I hope to establish in this section.

Have you ever found yourself saying, "We just don't play well together." Or, "I always seem to play well with him." The reason for this is no accident. Most people define why they do or don't play well with certain players based on strokes or styles of play (baseliner, net rusher, deuce court vs. ad court player, etc.), but this is only part of the reason. If Player A is out of position because she is not comfortable playing from a certain area of the court, it's now up to Player A's partner to adjust her positioning and shot selection to accommodate. As a result, "We just don't play well together." On the flip side, if both players are positioned well and can execute shots from those positions, they have a much higher probability of success, "I always seem to play well with him."

If you really want to improve as a doubles player, honor your team's formation by being positioned in the correct place regardless of your own comfort zone. To honor your team's formation, you need to hit your shots to the targets that contribute to that formation's success. If you feel you are unable to hit your shots to those targets, then you know what strokes you need to practice. Let me clarify that priority list here:

1. Positioning
2. Targets
3. Strokes

Does that order seem backward to you? What do you typically work on the most in practice sessions? Stroke mechanics are usually focused on the most, followed by hitting those strokes to particular targets. Positioning is then covered. Why? When anyone first learns to play tennis, initially they need to learn how to hit the ball (strokes), then learn how to aim their strokes (targets), followed by where to stand on the doubles court (positioning). In other words:

1. Strokes
2. Targets
3. Positioning

Working on strokes and targets is an ongoing progression no matter how advanced a player gets, and those practice sessions should primarily be done on an individual basis with a teaching pro. But why hit those strokes to particular targets? Why stand on various spots on the court? Eventually, the priority list needs to shift and team formations should be put first in order to answer these questions. Remember, the goal here is for you to improve as a doubles player, not just as a tennis player.

If you have been playing doubles for years, ask yourself how much attention you place on team positioning. Is your priority list the same as it was when you first learned to play? If so, commit your strokes and targets to complementing your team's formation and make sure you and your partner are on the same page. Let me address the importance of this priority list with an example. Have you ever been at a tennis match and it quickly became clear that one doubles team was much better than the other, only to find out later that the "better" team was losing badly? The reason for this is because our first instinct is to evaluate playing level based on stroke mechanics. Please understand, I am not saying that good strokes don't help win matches. It just can't be the primary focus during doubles matches.

In this segment, we will explore the formational options available to a doubles team, clearly define each player's responsibilities regarding positioning and shot selection, and state why each option can be useful. By the end, I hope that you can see which positioning options you execute well, and which ones need work. This is your first comfort zone challenge. You might not be comfortable in each position within the following formations, but it's important that you understand them all so you will know your responsibilities if you find yourself in an uncomfortable position. In addition, if you and your partner recognize that a certain formation would work well against a particular opponent, you need to be willing to execute that formation even if that area of the court is not within your comfort zone.

It is important to point out that each of the formations are broken down and analyzed individually. However, you may be required to execute several formations within a given point. Since you can't control where your opponent hits the ball, you can't always control which formation you are in. Therefore, you need to be prepared to fulfill your positional responsibilities, regardless of how many formations are required of you and your partner throughout a point.

I would like you to remember two major themes and apply them to all of the formations as each is broken down into greater specifics.

1. The player crosscourt from the ball needs to think of themself as the "Set-up Player," and the person down-the-line from the ball needs to think of themself as the "Finisher."

2. The Finisher should be closer to the net than the Set-up Player. This concept is very important to understand because shot selections made within each formation are designed to fulfill the role of the Set-up Player and Finisher. Remember that as we begin to break down the different formations.

Lastly, I can't stress enough the importance of **team** formations. You may look at a formation and want to do it because it's comfortable for you. But, what about your partner? How does that formation affect their game? Is that a smart formation to use based on your opponents' strengths and weaknesses? Be sure you are deciding together the formation(s) that maximizes your strengths as a team and/or your opponents' weaknesses.

TRADITIONAL FORMATIONS

There are three traditional formations in doubles that, for the most part, will dominate court positioning. These will be discussed first before breaking down the specialty formations.

Chapter 1

1-Up, 1-Back on Both Sides

General Overview

This formation involves one player on each side of the net being at the baseline, crosscourt from each other, and their partner being at the net *(Diagram 1)*. This is one of the most common formations in doubles, as most points begin this way.

Many teaching pros will teach their students to rush the net quickly to get out of this formation in an effort to control the net. However, rushing the net is not the only way to win. With the rapid improvement in racquet and string technology, players at every level are finding that they can have success with one player (or even both players) staying at the baseline. Even at the professional level, some players either stay back at the baseline strategically or because their opponents force them to stay back (possibly because the serve is so fast that they can't move into the net behind their return). This means that players can't and don't have to rush forward simply because they want to control the net at all costs. There must be more thought put into it than that, and you may find that staying at the baseline for longer periods of time can work for you.

In Diagram 1, Players A and D are crosscourt from each other at the baseline while Players B and C are crosscourt from each other at the net. Player B is currently closer to the net than Player C, indicating that Team AB is serving. First, let's discuss the movement of the players within this formation and then identify each player's responsibilities.

After Player A serves, the returner (Player D) returns the ball crosscourt back to Player A. At this point, Player B should move defensively back to the service line close to the "T," and Player C should move offensively forward toward the net *(Diagram 2)*. As Player A successfully hits a groundstroke crosscourt, Players B and C should move again to where they were originally in Diagram 1. As this crosscourt exchange continues from the baseline, the net players will continue to move forward offensively and backward defensively until the crosscourt groundstroke pattern changes.

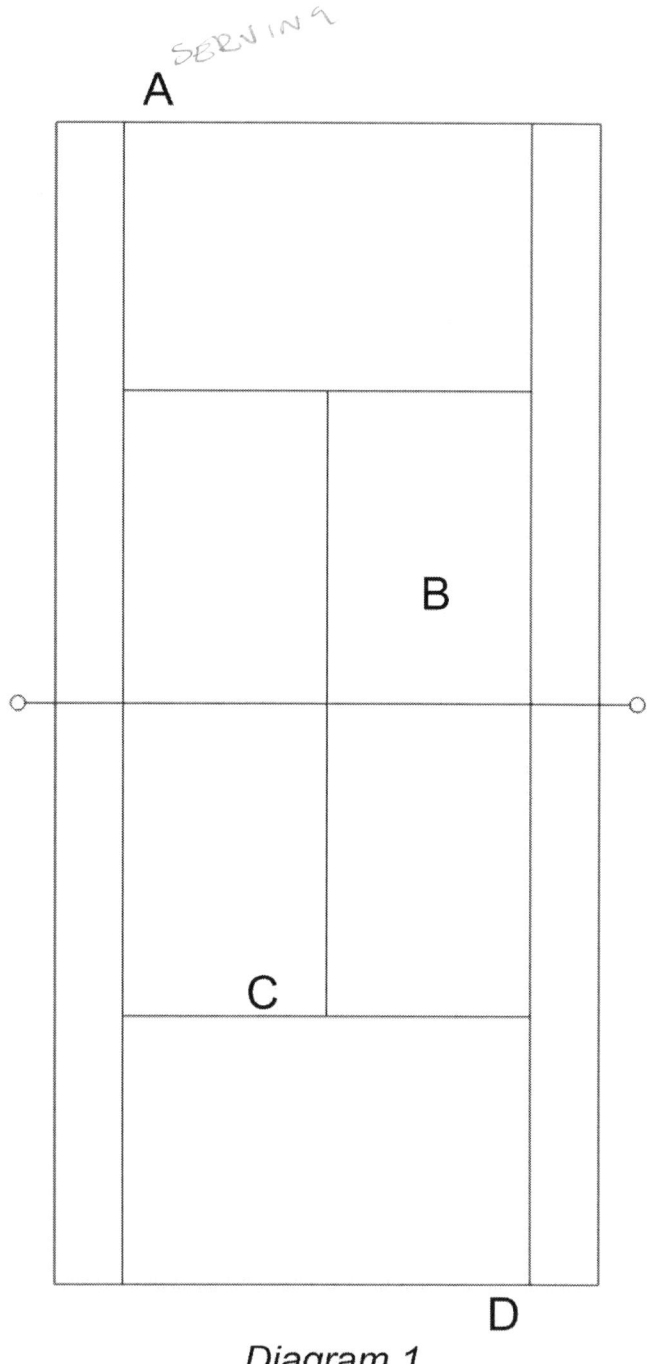

Diagram 1

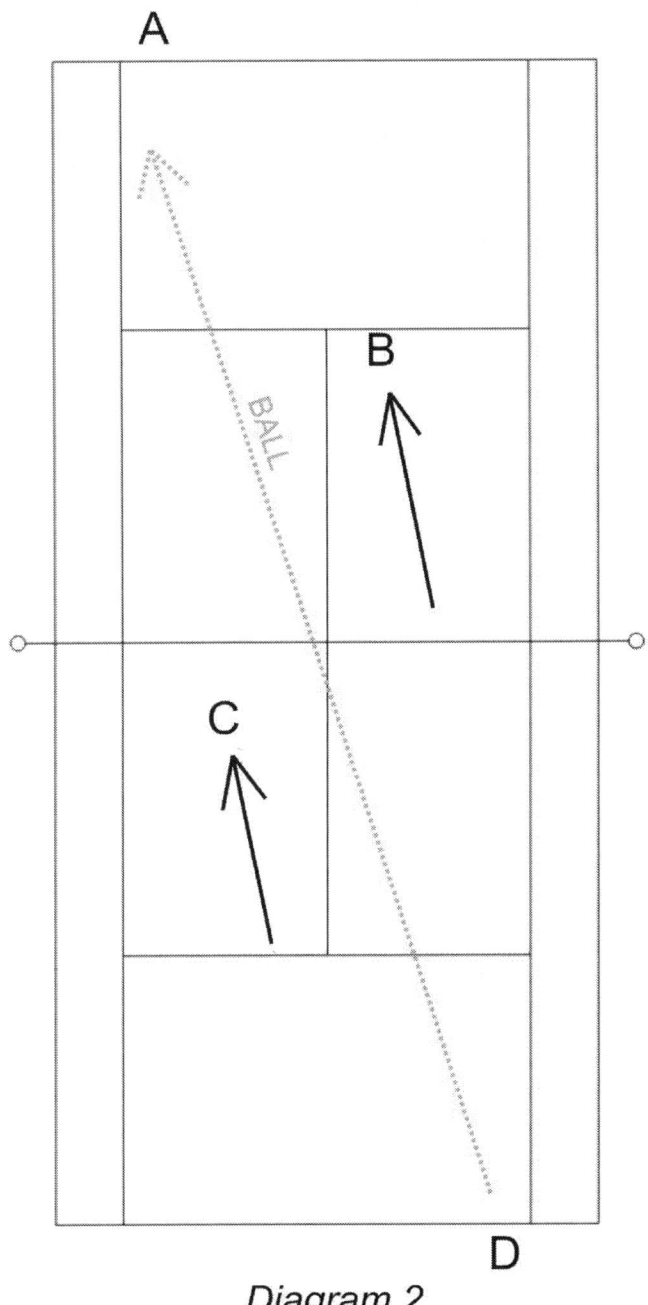

Diagram 2

Player A

As the serve is hit, Player A decides to stay back at the baseline to continue the point. Being crosscourt from the ball, Player A is the Set-up Player. This means that Player A's job is to choose shots that give Player B, the Finisher, a chance to finish the point with a winning volley. What are those shots? Crosscourt is the best option, as this gives Player B the best chance to hit a finishing volley. Obviously, there are more shot options available to Player A than just crosscourt. He might choose to go for a down-the-line shot past Player C or lob over Player C. Those are viable options depending on the situation. But, they don't set up Player B to finish the point. Remember, we are building a team foundation first, which means we need to stick to the theme of Set-up Player and Finisher.

Even though crosscourt might seem too simplistic to some of you, there are a few options as to where exactly Player A can hit crosscourt to set up Player B. A penetrating deep crosscourt shot definitely sets up Player B as this shot pushes Player D backward, which creates a weak reply for Player B to finish. A short and low crosscourt slice can set up Player B as well, as this will cause Player D to have to run forward and reach for the ball, making it difficult to keep the ball away from Player B's finishing volley. One other option is for Player A to hit a short-angle crosscourt shot with heavy topspin to pull Player D off the court. While this last choice can sometimes create additional angles for Player D to exploit, if Player B honors the formation and moves correctly, Team AB should win these points most of the time. Lastly, because Player B is moving forward offensively as Player A's shot travels crosscourt, Player A needs to be ready to cover all lobs.

To recap, Player A should:

- Hit offensively crosscourt.
- Keep the ball away from the opposing net player (Player C).
- Be ready to cover the lob over Player B's head.

Player B

Starting the point again, Player A serves the ball. Player B is already positioned close to the net, laterally near the center of the service box. As the serve travels past Player B, he needs to follow the ball. Following the ball sounds straightforward enough, but it is rarely done correctly. When most players in Player B's position follow the ball, they end up moving sideways toward the alley or toward the middle *(Diagram 3)*. Moving this way leaves too many openings and makes it too easy for Player D to get the ball around Player B. The best and simplest way I have found to define following the ball is to instead say "follow the contact." In other words, wherever Player D is going to make contact with the ball, Player B needs to draw a straight line between his position and his opponent's anticipated contact point, and then move on that line, getting very close to the net *(Diagram 4)*. By following the contact close to the net, Player B now has the best possible chance to cut off the next shot hit by Player D, whether he hits the ball crosscourt or down-the-line. You might ask, "But, if I get too close to the net, won't I get lobbed?" You might. But, whose job is it to cover that lob? Reread Player A's bullet point responsibilities. If you are both covering the lob, you are no longer honoring the formation. Remember, this is fundamental. If your team needs to adjust as the match progresses, you should make the adjustment together. But, start here.

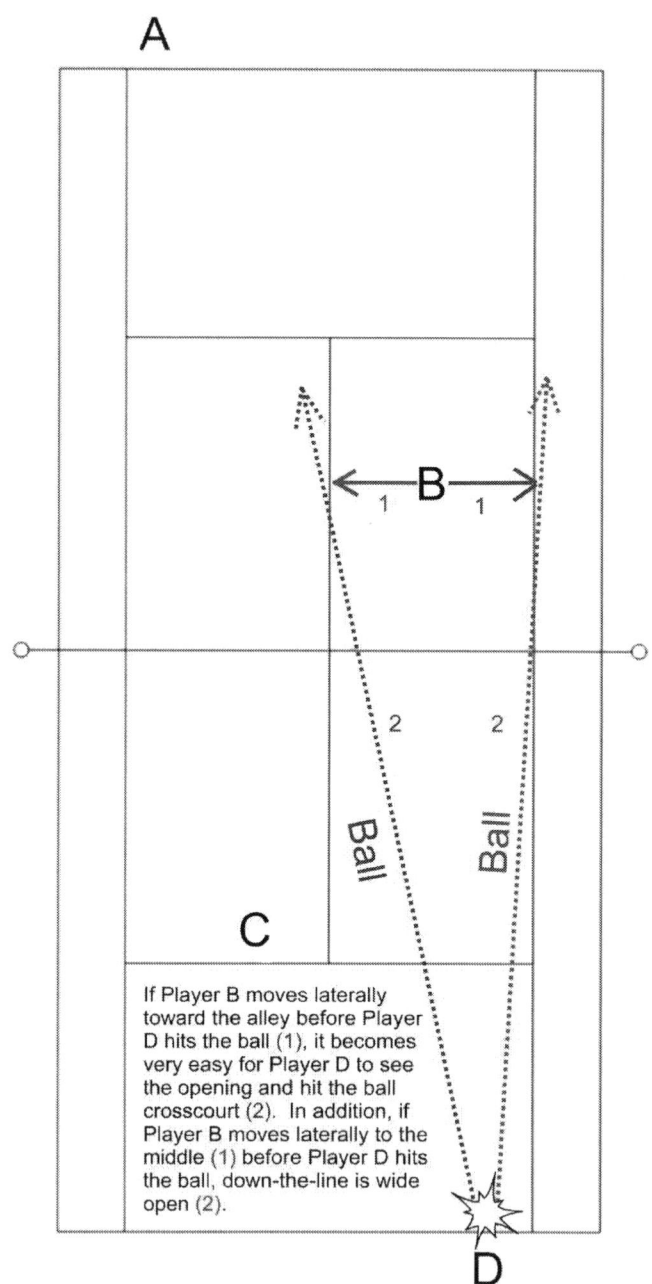

If Player B moves laterally toward the alley before Player D hits the ball (1), it becomes very easy for Player D to see the opening and hit the ball crosscourt (2). In addition, if Player B moves laterally to the middle (1) before Player D hits the ball, down-the-line is wide open (2).

Diagram 3

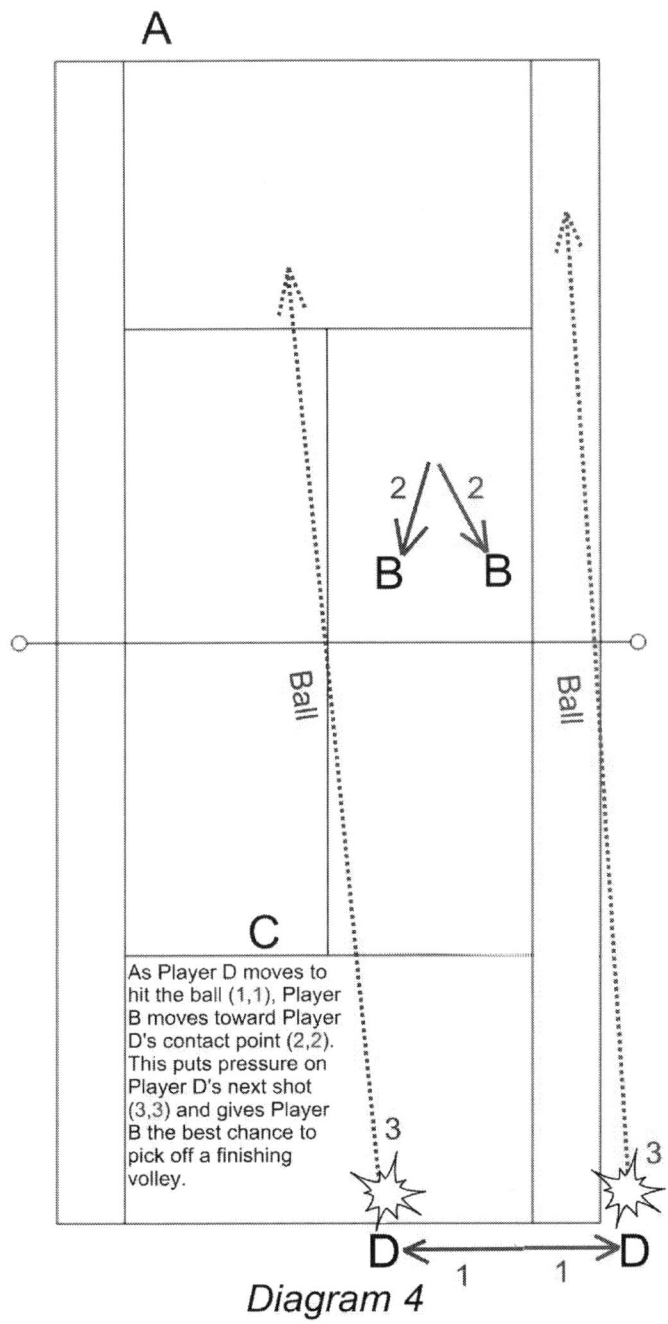

As Player D moves to hit the ball (1,1), Player B moves toward Player D's contact point (2,2). This puts pressure on Player D's next shot (3,3) and gives Player B the best chance to pick off a finishing volley.

Diagram 4

One last point. When Player B is repeatedly lobbed, most players in that position will adjust by backing off the net to prevent the lob. Before backing off the net, first be sure to evaluate the shot Player A hit immediately before the lob. Chances are, it was not a good enough shot, and it allowed Player D to send up the lob. Try to execute that shot better before adjusting the formation.

It is important to note here that as Player D strikes the ball, Player B needs to be completely balanced by using a proper split step. Many times, net players like Player B are still moving as their opponent strikes the ball, making it extremely difficult to change direction and cut off angles. Some players also guess where their opponent might hit the ball and lean too early to the middle or the alley. Leaning, shifting, or running while your opponent is hitting the ball reduces your ability to honor your responsibilities within a given formation and causes confusion for a doubles team.

Getting back to the point in progress, if Player D successfully hits the ball crosscourt past Player B, Player B needs to move quickly to the service line near the "T" *(Diagram 2)*. The reason why Player B wants to be near the "T" is because they are preparing to defend against Player C's offensive volley in the event that Player A hits the ball in Player C's direction. This position allows Player B to cut off as much of the court as possible from Player C and stay in the point *(Diagram 5)*. If Player A successfully hits the ball crosscourt back to Player D, Player B should again follow the contact and get close to the net. This movement pattern stays the same if the crosscourt exchange between Player A and Player D continues.

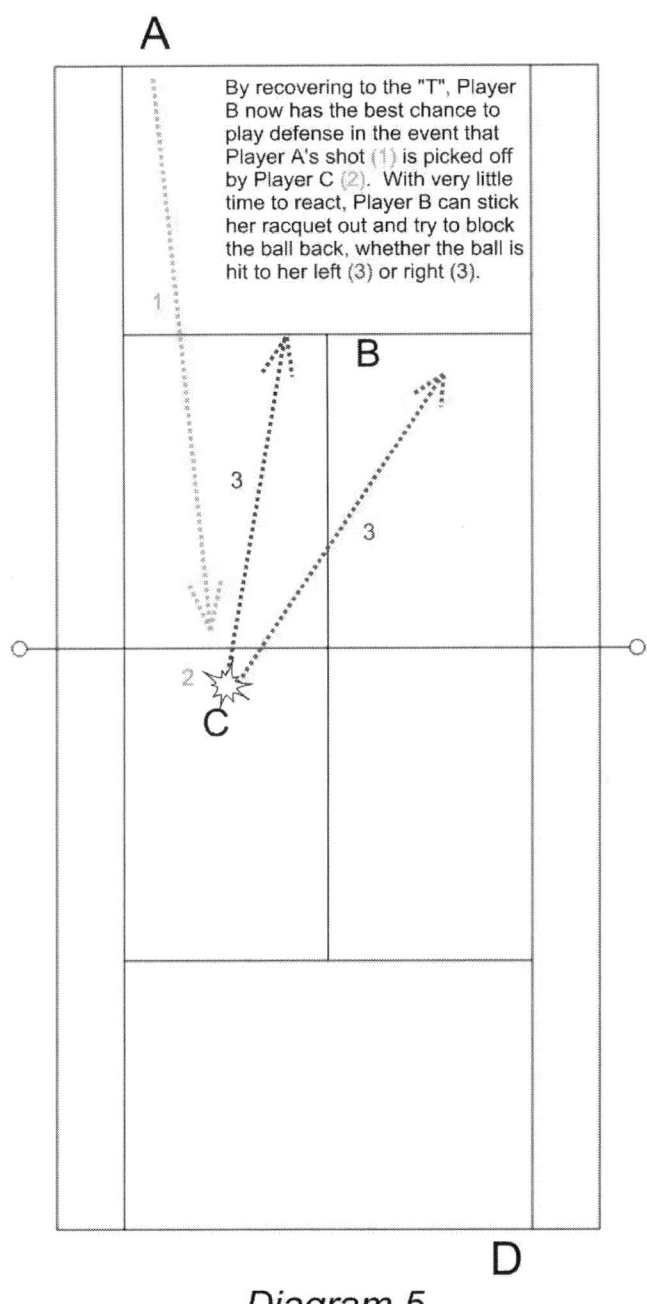

By recovering to the "T", Player B now has the best chance to play defense in the event that Player A's shot (1) is picked off by Player C (2). With very little time to react, Player B can stick her racquet out and try to block the ball back, whether the ball is hit to her left (3) or right (3).

Diagram 5

To recap, Player B should:

- "Follow the contact" close to the net to finish volleys.
- Retreat defensively near the "T."
- Offensively cover the alley and most of the middle.
- Ignore the lob until it becomes necessary to adjust as a team.

Player C

Essentially, Player C's responsibilities are the same as Player B's. The primary difference is that Player B starts the point in an offensive position (server's partner) while Player C starts in a defensive position (returner's partner).

Player D

Player D is the returner in the example used in this chapter. The same principles used to describe Player A's responsibilities should be applied to Player D. Even though Player D is returning serve, which sometimes gives this player less initial control of the point, Player D should still be considered the Set-up Player and concentrate on hitting an effective crosscourt return followed by crosscourt shots that allow Player C to finish the point with a volley.

Drills for Practice

One drill I like to use to practice this formation involves first positioning four players of equal ability in each of the four positions described above. The net players will set down their racquets off to the side of the court. The two baseline players will rally crosscourt while the net players practice following the contact offensively forward and then defensively back near the "T." If done correctly, both net players should move in sync (one forward and one backward) and use the split step to stop as each ball is struck by a baseliner. Depending on your quickness, you may find it difficult to keep up with the speed of the crosscourt rally at first. If you are simply unable to keep up, make sure you are at least recovering to the "T." What most players realize after doing this drill is that the net players should be working much harder physically than the baseliners.

After doing this correctly for several minutes, the net players can pick up their racquets and try to pick off volleys. One tip I have for net players learning this movement is to start by first paying attention to your movement and timing. Are you close to the net when you should be? Are you near the "T" when you should be? Also, be aware that you might be tempted as a Finisher to move across the middle a lot because you find yourself so close to the net. The payoff can be that you are able to finish points with an offensive volley, but if you fail to get to the ball in time and it travels to your partner at the baseline before you can get back to the "T," you will not be able to defend against the opposing net player, especially if they are moving forward with the ball (Diagram 6).

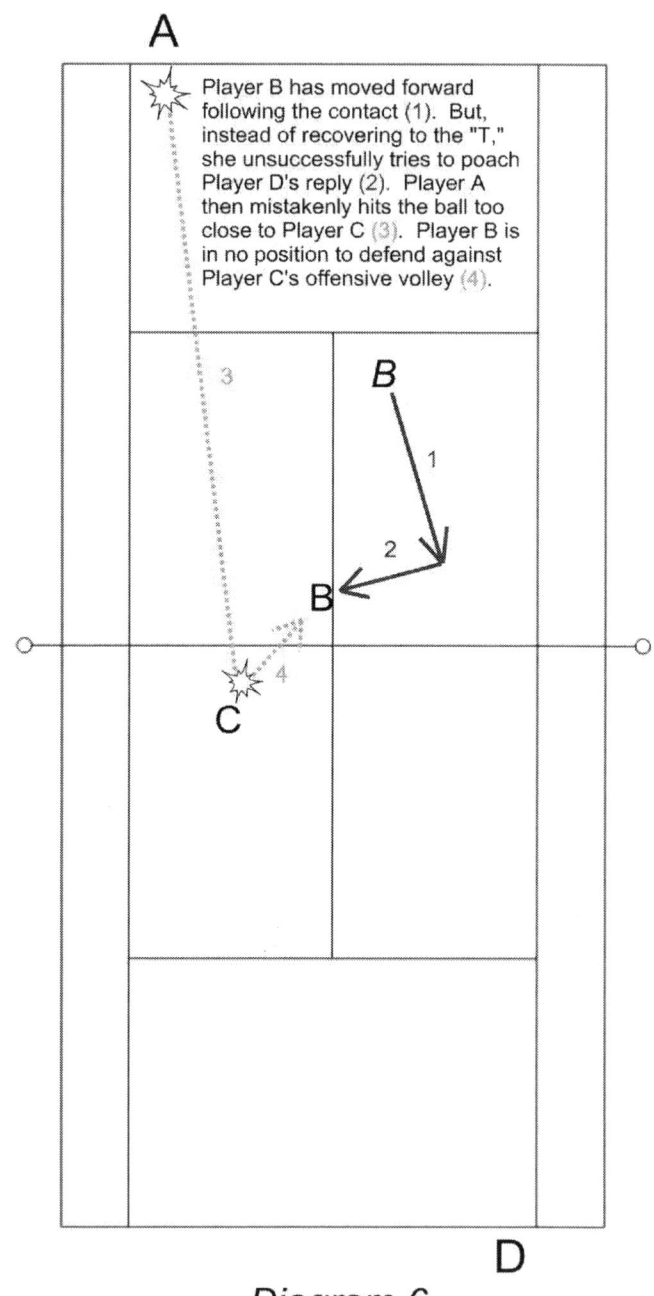

Player B has moved forward following the contact (1). But, instead of recovering to the "T," she unsuccessfully tries to poach Player D's reply (2). Player A then mistakenly hits the ball too close to Player C (3). Player B is in no position to defend against Player C's offensive volley (4).

Diagram 6

What to Watch For: 4.0 and Above

At higher levels of play, the serve and return quality increases, so gaining control of a point early becomes extremely important. Remember that the goal of this formation is for the crosscourt baseliner to set up his or her partner to finish the point. The server has the first opportunity to do this by effectively executing the serve. If the server has an ineffective serve, or if the server is missing a high number of first serves and has to then hit a lot of slower second serves, the returner now can set up his or her partner with an offensive return.

Shots tend to get hit harder at higher levels of play, which means that net players need to move quicker as they follow the contact forward and then move back to the "T." Higher-level players also can add extra spin and/or power, take pace off the ball when appropriate, and place their shots with better accuracy. This makes it imperative for net players to be positioned in the right place and on balance. If not, you can be sure that higher-level opponents will exploit your poor positioning and body control.

Overall, 1-up, 1-back on both sides is less common at levels 4.5 and above, as at least one team is trying to offensively get both players up to the net. If you don't find you or your opponents playing in the 1-up, 1-back on both sides formation very often, just be sure you honor your positioning responsibilities when it happens so you and your partner are on the same page.

What to Watch For: 3.5 and Below

At this level, the ball is typically hit slower and higher. Lobs are much more prevalent because players typically don't have the confidence to hit the ball hard and in the court. In addition, many players at lower levels don't definitively know where to hit the ball. In a moment of uncertainty and/or confusion, the tendency is to lob it up to be safe. As a result, sometimes the net player might charge offensively to try to finish a point only to be lobbed over time and time again. When this happens, avoid abandoning the team formation by having the net player stand only at the service line to prevent the lob, which is what many players do at this level. Instead, see if the baseline player can execute a good enough shot that doesn't allow the opposing baseliner to lob. I always tell my students to try to improve execution before adjusting positioning and/or strategy. The baseline player might need to drive the ball deeper or drop it low and short (both crosscourt). If executing these shots better is not an option—you now know what shots you need to practice—you can then adjust to a different formation or adjust your positioning within the 1-up, 1-back formation.

Chapter 2

1-Up, 1-Back on One Side, 2-Up on the Other Side

General Overview

1-Up, 1-Back on one side, 2-Up on the other is a very common setup in which one team has both players at the net while the other team has one player at the net and one player at the baseline *(Diagram 7)*. As you can see in the diagram, Player D has been able to approach the net by hitting the ball crosscourt to Player A. Players A and D are the Set-up Players because they are crosscourt from the ball. Players B and C are the Finishers because they are down-the-line from the ball. I describe Player B's position here as being the hot seat because he will either be put in an extremely offensive or defensive position, depending on the quality of Player A's groundstroke. In addition, Player C is dependent on Player D hitting a high-quality approach shot because, while having both players at the net can prove to be very offensive, it can also make a doubles team vulnerable to a variety of shots if they're not positioned properly and/or don't execute a good enough approach shot.

One term that becomes very important to understand as we move into the details of this formation is to "stagger." Staggering involves having both players at the net but positioned at different distances from the net. The Finisher (down-the-line from the ball) should be close to the net, and the Set-up Player (crosscourt from the ball) should be at the service line *(Diagram 7)*.

As Player D hits the approach shot crosscourt, he moves forward and stops (using the split step) at the service line. Player D will now stay at the service line for the remainder of the point if the crosscourt pattern continues. "What?! Stay at the service line?! That's not what

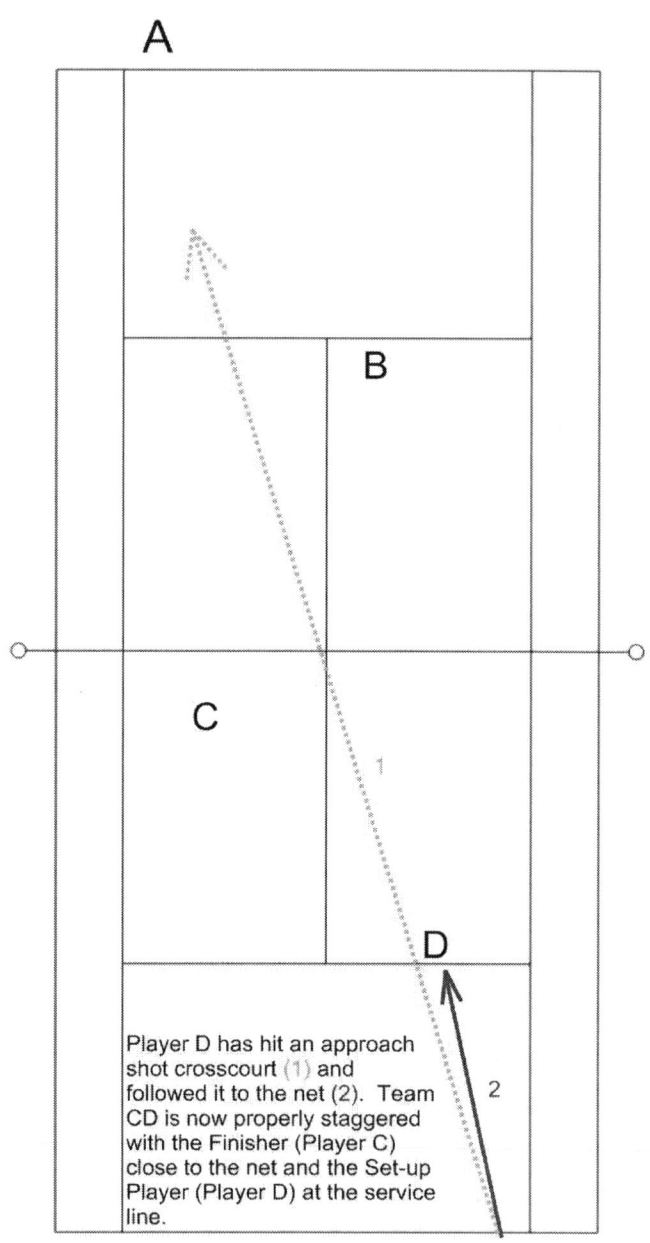

Player D has hit an approach shot crosscourt (1) and followed it to the net (2). Team CD is now properly staggered with the Finisher (Player C) close to the net and the Set-up Player (Player D) at the service line.

Diagram 7

I have been taught in all the clinics I have taken!" I know. This goes against conventional wisdom when it comes to net positioning. Let me guess what you might have heard in the past. "You need to move forward together like a wall," "Pretend you have a rope tied between you and your partner so you follow the ball and move together at the net." Or, "CLOSE! CLOSE! CLOSE!" The fact of the matter is that playing points with this mindset will leave you extremely frustrated because you will never be able to cover all the angles as a team. And, playing as a team is what we are trying to move toward, which starts with positioning yourselves as a team. Let's discuss each player's responsibilities so this formation can become clearer.

Player A

As Player D approaches the net, this naturally applies pressure to Player A. This pressure is felt because Player A now must make sure he hits a good enough shot that Team CD can't put the next ball away. Let's examine Player A's basic shot selection options here:

1. Hit the ball low crosscourt.
2. Hit the ball down-the-line.
3. Lob.

You might read those and wonder why down the middle is not listed. "Doesn't down the middle solve the riddle?" It does if both opposing net players are off the net and not properly staggered. Down-the-line is also open if Player C is not properly staggered *(Diagram 8)*. If Team CD is properly staggered, down the middle should get picked off by Player C and is not a good option.

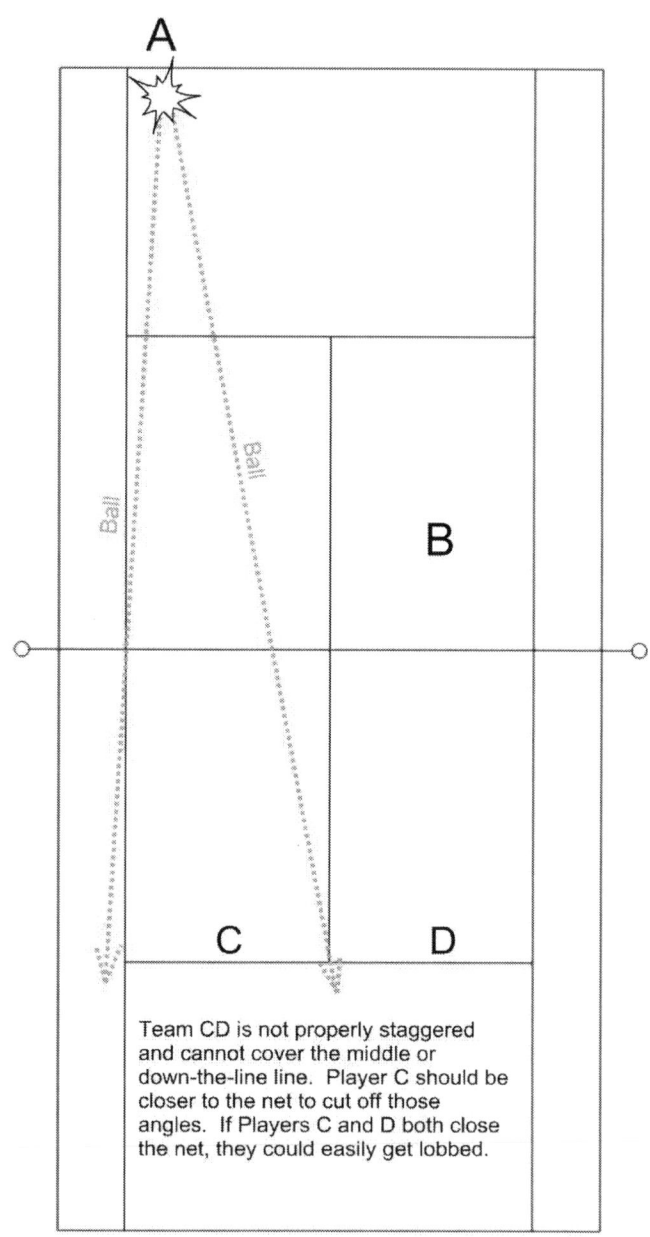

Team CD is not properly staggered and cannot cover the middle or down-the-line line. Player C should be closer to the net to cut off those angles. If Players C and D both close the net, they could easily get lobbed.

Diagram 8

If Player A chooses not to lob, the number one priority should be hitting the ball low over the net, regardless of the lateral target. Net players are most offensive if they are given a high volley opportunity. It is also wise for Player A to only lob sparingly and for a strategic reason. Many players hit a lob here because they feel pressure and are in a state of confusion or panic and don't know what else to do. Players need to program themselves to aim low over the net first when unsure and do their best to execute the shot. Remember, even though Player D has approached the net, Player A is still the Set-up Player for Player B and needs to think of crosscourt options to honor the formation. What most players in Player A's position don't realize is that a lob here not only eliminates the team formation, but it also takes their partner out of a potentially offensive position. Let's look at two points played out based on Player A's choice of shot:

Scenario One: Player A Lobs

Player A decides to lob. As the lob goes up in the air, Player B must either stay at the service line or move back to the baseline to defend against an overhead. If the lob successfully goes over their opponent's heads, Player B will still be unable to move in and close the net, because the next likely shot their opponent will hit back will be another lob.

> *Side note: I have seen many net players close the net after their partner hits a deep lob, only to watch their opponent lob the ball back over their head. Throughout the course of the match, the baseline player is constantly running back and forth along the baseline retrieving lobs while the net player watches the ball going back and forth over their head. This is not a very fun way to spend a day of tennis.*

Back to the point in progress. With Player B staying at the service line, Team AB now hopes that their opponent hits a short lob, so an overhead opportunity presents itself to Player B. If the lob coming back is hit high and deep, another lob will likely need to be hit back. And so on. Player A is not honoring his role as the Set-up Player by choosing to lob, and Player B has no real opportunity to finish the point.

Scenario Two: Player A Hits the Ball Low Crosscourt

Player A hits the ball low over the net at Player D's feet. When this happens, Player B can now look to move closer to the net to try to pick off his opponent's next shot. Even if Player A doesn't hit it directly to Player D's feet, if the ball travels low over the net, Player B can try to play more offensively. If Player B can't move in and pick off a volley because Player D handles the low volley well and places it crosscourt, Player A can try to hit another low ball to set up Player B again. And so on. Player A is now honoring his role as the Set-up Player and Player B can look to finish.

Which scenario sounds more offensive to you? Definitely, Scenario Two. Don't misunderstand me. There are times when hitting a lob or down-the-line shot is very smart and/or necessary. For starters, I tell my students that a good rule of thumb is to choose to hit the specialty shots (lobs, down-the-lines, etc.) when you firmly believe that you can win the point outright with that shot. If you are uncertain, honor your responsibilities as the Set-up Player by choosing crosscourt targets. Keep in mind, when Player A chooses to lob or hit down-the-line, Player B doesn't know that Player A has decided to do this until well after the ball is struck, limiting his time to appropriately react. I have seen many points played out where Player A fires a ball down-the-line at Player C only to have Player C put a volley away through the middle of the court before Player B can even react *(Diagram 9)*, which is not fundamental team doubles. What I want everyone reading this book (I'm sorry, studying this book) to understand is that establishing the fundamental formations and making shot selections as a team that enhance those formations should be the trunk and root system of your doubles. All other specialty shots, targets, and lesser-known formations are the limbs that branch off that trunk and root system.

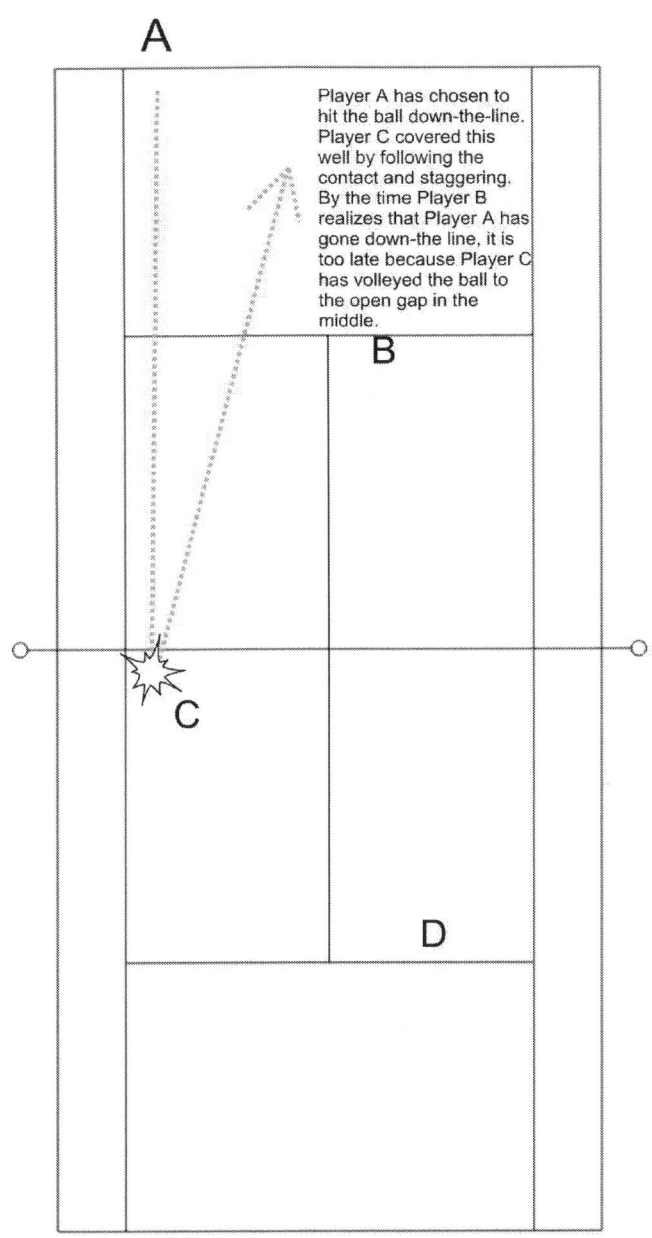

A

Player A has chosen to hit the ball down-the-line. Player C covered this well by following the contact and staggering. By the time Player B realizes that Player A has gone down-the line, it is too late because Player C has volleyed the ball to the open gap in the middle.

B

C

D

Diagram 9

To recap, Player A should:

- Aim low over the net first.
- Keep the ball crosscourt away from Player C and ideally at Player D's feet to honor the formation.
- Use lobs, down-the-lines, and specialty shots/targets only when necessary or as a way to end points.

Player B

As stated earlier, when Player D approaches the net, Player B is now in the "hot seat." Player B is completely dependent on Player A hitting a good enough shot so that Player C or D can't finish a volley. How do we define a good enough shot? First, Player A must hit the ball low over the net. If this is done, offense will be extremely limited for Team CD regardless of which player hits the volley. However, if Player A makes the mistake of hitting the ball too high, Player B will now be target practice for either Player C or D. Secondly, as the Set-up Player, Player A should try to aim crosscourt. The pinnacle is for Player A to hit the ball at Player D's feet. This target best sets up Player B to take an offensive position and finish a volley.

The reality for Player B is that as Player A hits the ball and it travels crosscourt to Player D's feet, there is very little time to move forward to hit an offensive volley. Player B needs to be sure that Player C is not going to cut off Player A's shot before moving closer to the net. However, as soon as Player B recognizes that the ball is going to Player D's feet, the opportunity to move forward needs to be seized by Player B to cut off Player D's available angles and put a volley away *(Diagram 10)*. If Player B can't move in or is not able to hit a volley, she needs to stay at the service line near the "T" and wait for an opportunity to close the net, while also staying prepared to defend from that position. If you find yourself playing a match where the ball is being hit extremely hard and you are in Player B's position, you may not even have time to close the net before Player D hits the volley. In this case, don't try to move before Player D hits the volley. Just be ready to cut off Player D's volley if she floats it up defensively.

To recap, Player B should:

- Remain at the "T" until a low crosscourt shot is hit by their partner.
- When the ball is hit low and crosscourt, try to close the net to put away a volley.
- Recover to the "T" to defend and wait for another opportunity to move forward if a finishing volley is not available.

Player C

In Chapter 1, we learned that it is the net player's responsibility in the 1-up, 1-back on both sides scenario to move forward as the ball travels crosscourt toward the opposing baseliner and then back to the "T" as the ball travels crosscourt toward the baseline partner. The difference in this formation is that as Player D approaches the net, Player C no longer needs to recover to the "T." If Player C did recover to the "T," then Team CD would now have both players at the service line and no longer be properly staggered at the net. As a result, they would be unable to cover the angles appropriately *(Diagram 8)*. To correctly honor this formation, Player C needs to remain close to the net when Player D approaches and laterally "follow the contact," depending on where Player A contacts the ball. Then, she should look to cut off the next possible volley. If Player A's shot successfully goes back to Player D, Player C needs to remain close to the net and depend on Player D to hit a quality crosscourt volley to reset the sequence.

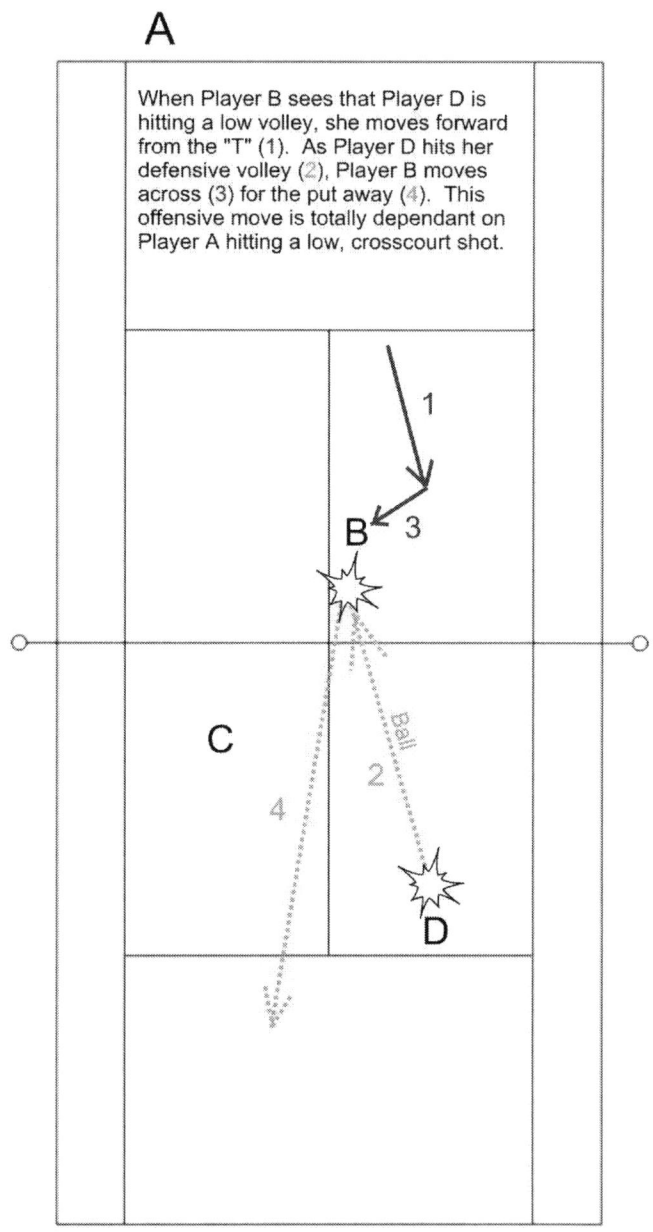

When Player B sees that Player D is hitting a low volley, she moves forward from the "T" (1). As Player D hits her defensive volley (2), Player B moves across (3) for the put away (4). This offensive move is totally dependant on Player A hitting a low, crosscourt shot.

Diagram 10

To recap, Player C should:

- Stay close to the net as Player D approaches the net.
- Cover the alley and most of the middle by "following the contact."
- Ignore the lob.

Player D

In the General Overview section for this formation, I stated that as Player D approaches, she should hit the approach shot and then remain at the service line for the remainder of the point. The reason why this is so important is because while Players C and D are both at the net, one of them needs to be prepared to cover the lob. Remember, Player C is supposed to close the net to cover the alley and most of the middle. The only way for this to happen is for Player C to move close to the net. Player D now has the responsibility of covering all lobs (unless one is hit so short that Player C can put an overhead away) and crosscourt out of Player C's reach *(Diagram 11)*. The only time Player D can move forward from the service line is if either Player A or B floats a high ball to Player D. As the ball floats in the air, Player D can run forward to offensively hit a winner before it drops below the net.

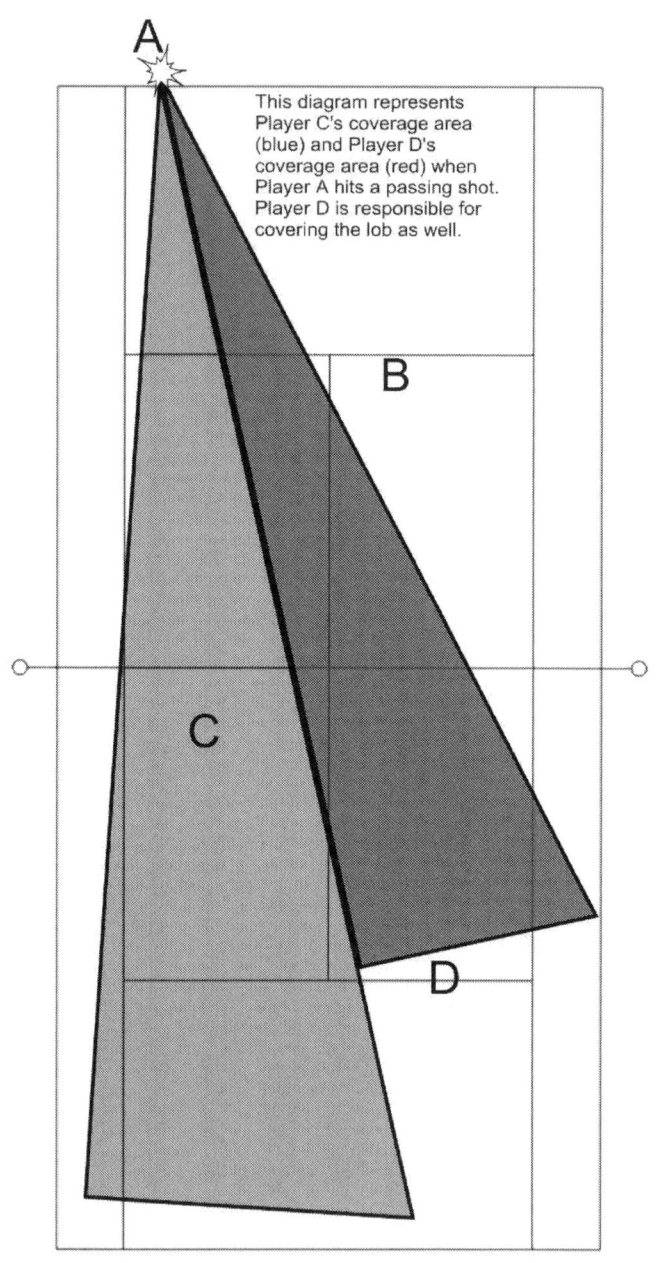

This diagram represents Player C's coverage area (blue) and Player D's coverage area (red) when Player A hits a passing shot. Player D is responsible for covering the lob as well.

Diagram 11

You might be thinking that it will be very difficult for Player D to cover her half of the court as well as all lobs. If you are, you are exactly right. This is why I highlight the importance of the approach shot. If the approach shot is hit well, Player A should have a much harder time producing offense. Consequently, Team CD should be able to stay on offense. If the approach shot is hit weak or poorly, Player D should be ready to run down a lob or dive for a volley. These are two drastically different directions that a point can take depending on that one shot.

If Player A hits Player D's approach shot back crosscourt, Player D's job is to volley the ball crosscourt to set up Player C. Player D can try to penetrate the volley deep or drop the volley short, both crosscourt. As long as Player A remains at the baseline and hits the ball crosscourt, Player D should continue to volley crosscourt until Player C can put away a volley or until the crosscourt pattern changes.

If Player A lobs one of Player D's shots down-the-line over Player C, Player D now has a quick decision to make. Let's discuss the two primary options available to Player D in this scenario:

1. If Player D chooses to let the lob bounce, she should run back to the baseline behind Player C, and Player C should switch to the other side of the court at the service line *(Diagram 12)*. We will discuss the details of the formation after Player D's next shot in a later chapter. For now, what is important to understand is that Player D has the opportunity to hit the ball down-the-line as many times as necessary before earning an approach shot, which would be hit down-the-line to Player A. Player D would then continue to close the net to try to put a volley away *(Diagram 13)*. Player D is now in an effective finishing position and Player C is the Set-up Player. This is what should be done in this scenario for Team CD to effectively return to their original team formation.

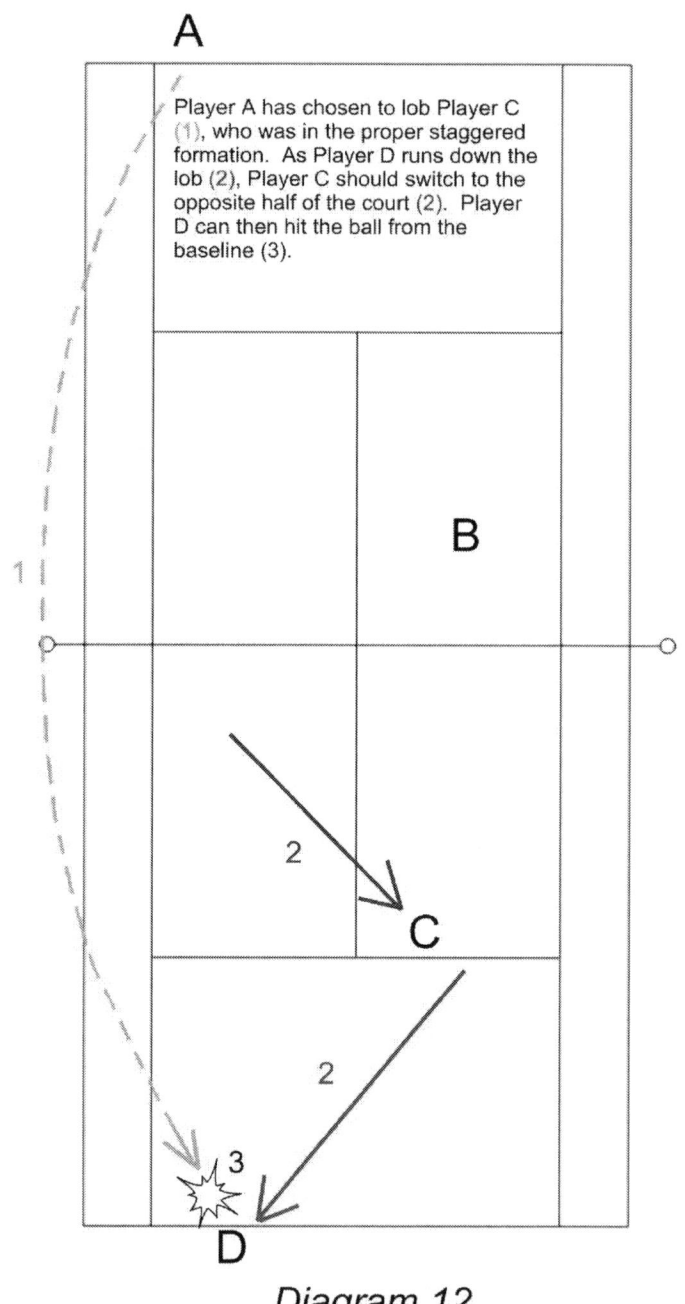

A

Player A has chosen to lob Player C
(1), who was in the proper staggered
formation. As Player D runs down the
lob (2), Player C should switch to the
opposite half of the court (2). Player
D can then hit the ball from the
baseline (3).

B

Diagram 12

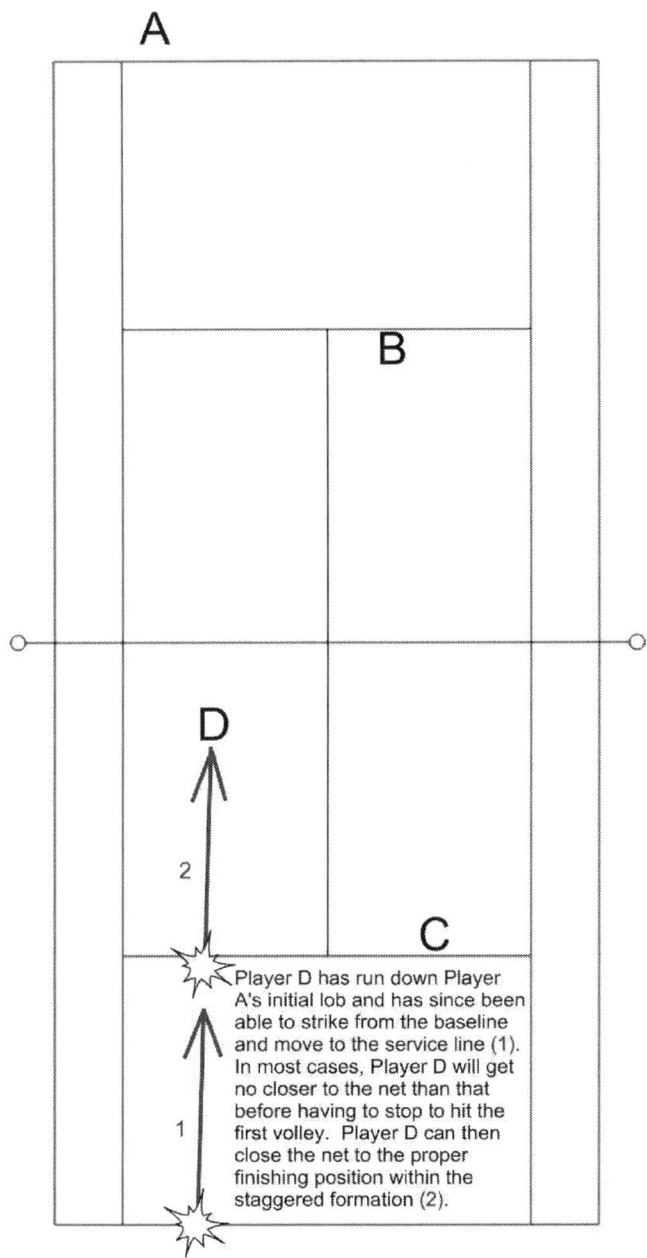

Player D has run down Player A's initial lob and has since been able to strike from the baseline and move to the service line (1). In most cases, Player D will get no closer to the net than that before having to stop to hit the first volley. Player D can then close the net to the proper finishing position within the staggered formation (2).

Diagram 13

2. Player D's second option is to move from the service line behind Player C and hit the ball out of the air as a high volley *(Diagram 14)*. Player D must be able to get there before the ball drops below shoulder level or else it must be bounced. This requires Player D to move extremely fast and is not always possible if there is not enough time to get there to execute the high volley. If Player D can get there in time, she should be able to hit the high volley down-the-line to the opposing baseliner and immediately close the net to take the offensive finishing position before the next shot. Player C's responsibility is to switch sides and move to the service line, just like in Scenario 1 *(Diagram 12)*. By taking the lob out of the air, Player D has helped Team CD to return to their original team formation in the quickest way possible.

It is important to point out here that both scenarios can be very effective depending on the strengths and weaknesses of Team CD. For example, if Player D prefers to be at the baseline but was drawn into the net by a short crosscourt shot by Player A, then Player D might like to let Player A's down-the-line lob bounce and then stay at the baseline to hit groundstrokes.

Another example would be this scenario in the deuce court versus the ad court. In Diagram 14, if Player D is right-handed, she would be hitting a high backhand volley, which can be more difficult for many players. Player D may choose to let the ball bounce when moving to the ad court, but take it out of the air as a forehand volley when she is moving to the deuce court.

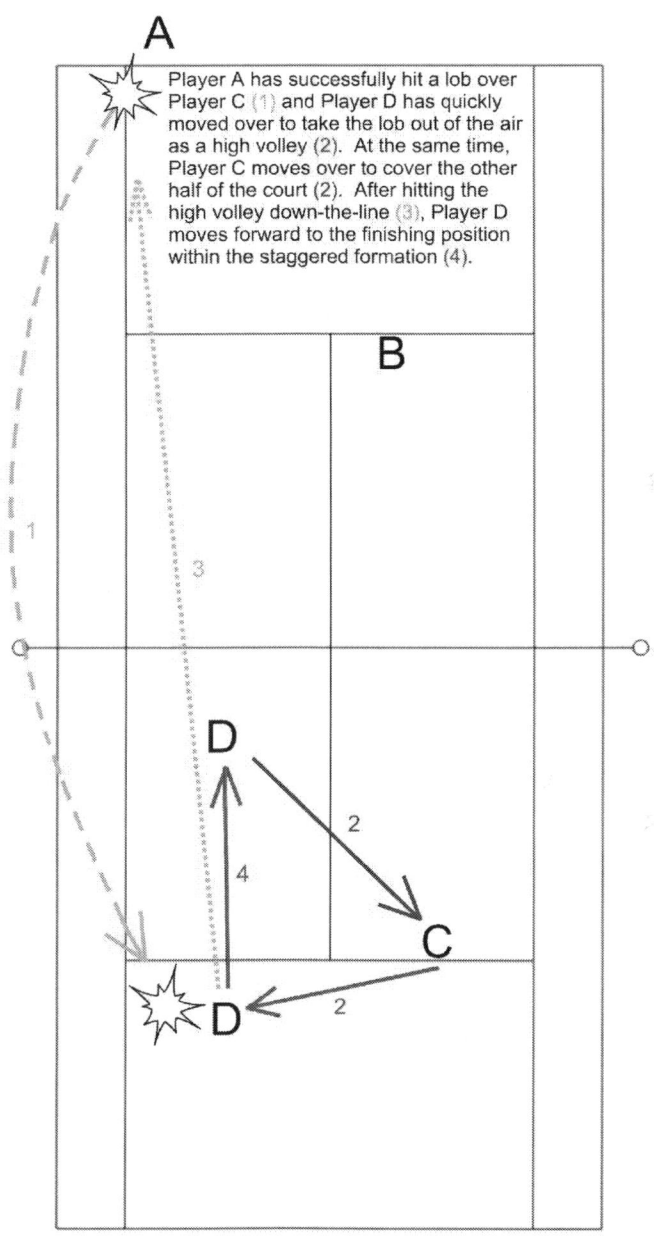

Player A has successfully hit a lob over Player C (1) and Player D has quickly moved over to take the lob out of the air as a high volley (2). At the same time, Player C moves over to cover the other half of the court (2). After hitting the high volley down-the-line (3), Player D moves forward to the finishing position within the staggered formation (4).

Diagram 14

One other important facet to taking the lob out of the air is that some players might find that they are quick enough to get under the ball and hit an overhead. As illustrated in Diagram 14, it would be necessary for Player D to be left-handed to get an overhead. If the same scenario was played out with the point beginning in the ad court, then Player D could take the lob as an overhead as a right-handed player.

To recap, Player D should:

- Move in to the service line and stay there to effectively stagger.
- Be prepared to cover the crosscourt shot as well as all lobs.
- Hit the ball crosscourt to set up Player C.
- Decide quickly to take lobs out of the air as a high volley, overhead, or let them bounce.

Drills for Practice

One drill I like to use to practice this formation can be done with either three or four players on the court. Two players on one side are properly staggered at the net while the other side has one player back at the baseline with or without a partner at the net. Using the diagram from above, Player D will feed in a ball crosscourt to Player A. Player A will then hit the ball crosscourt to Player D, who will then volley the ball back to Player A. Player A will then lob the ball down-the-line over Player C. Player D will then decide to either let the lob bounce or take it out of the air. The point can then be played out from there.

It is possible to execute several variations of this drill. One variation is to eliminate lobs to give Players A and D a chance to practice the high-percentage crosscourt shots. This also gives Players B and C a chance to get involved and pick off volleys.

Another variation I like to practice is where Player A alternates between hitting the groundstroke crosscourt and then lobbing down-the-line. The lobs are taken out of the air continuously and hit down-the-line. The result is that Player D covers the first lob and then closes the net while Player C switches to the service line to Player D's original position (Diagram 14). Then, Player C volleys the next crosscourt shot. Lastly, Player C covers the lob and closes the net while Player D switches to the service line, and so on. Due to the continued accuracy needed to execute this drill, I usually put myself in as Player A. This is a good example of how helpful it is to have a seasoned teaching pro on the court. This drill allows Team CD to really get comfortable working together and maintaining proper staggered positions. Do this drill with Player A positioned in the deuce court for a period of time. Then, move Player A's position over to the ad court.

What to Watch for: 4.0 and Above

As the level of play increases from 4.0 to 4.5 and 5.0 and so on, staggering is usually done with both players moving slightly closer and closer to the net, especially Player D. The reason for this is because the ball is hit harder as the level increases, which makes it more difficult to routinely lob. As Player D moves to the net, the high-quality approach shot will more often dictate that a lob by Player A will be much more difficult to execute. In addition, overheads are hit extremely hard, and there is a greater ability by net players to quickly move back and snap a hard overhead. You might have seen high-level players airborne while smashing an overhead. This makes it necessary for lobs to be used more sparingly by Team AB and with great disguise. It is also important for Player D to try more often to take the lob out of the air. If the lob is bounced and then lobbed back at higher levels, the greater the chance of the opponent smashing an overhead. Each of these examples allows Team CD to close the net a little tighter than lower-level players.

What to Watch for: 3.5 and Below

As stated earlier, players at 3.5 and below tend to hit the ball slower and higher. The propensity of lobs at this level make Player D's approach shot even that much more important. If Player D comes in on a slow-moving approach shot and allows Player A to have time to decide on their next shot with little to no pressure, Team CD will more than likely scramble to retrieve Player A's next shot. Player D needs *to be sure that he approaches the net at the right time using the most effective shot possible. If a low-quality ball is hit by Player D, he should try to retreat to the baseline and look for a better opportunity to approach the net.*

Chapter 3

All Four Players Up at the Net

General Overview

My favorite formation! For all of you net rushers and thrill seekers, this scenario is for you. What is fun about this formation is that both teams are typically trying to move from the baseline to the net and then prove to be the more offensive team at the net. The result is a fast-paced exchange of volleys that can end up in a winner, an error, or one of the four players getting pegged with the ball...so much fun!

Side note: Getting hit with the ball is a part of tennis. Many players feel so guilty at the prospect of hitting their opponent that they actually miss the shot in an effort to keep the ball away from them. In all honesty, there are many times when it is smart to hit the ball at your opponent, and you should never feel guilty if you hit them. Obviously, you're not trying to hurt them (hopefully not). Apologizing for hitting them is appropriate. But if the same scenario presents itself later in the match and you believe it is strategically smart to do so, you should hit it at them again. If they don't like getting hit, then they either need to execute their previous shot better (they might have floated the ball up too high giving you a very offensive opportunity) or back off the net so they don't get hit.

It is important to go into detail about how to give yourself the best chance to succeed within this formation by explaining the best way to get into this position and also how to maximize your effectiveness once all four players have made it to the net.

For all four players to be at the net, one of the two teams had to get their baseline player in before the other team. This means that Chapters 1 and 2 would need to have been used before all four players could make it to the net, even if the concepts in those chapters are only being used for one shot. At high levels of doubles, you might see this happening within the first two shots of a point. The server comes in immediately behind their serve (serve and volley), and the returner comes in behind their return. Even if it takes longer for this scenario to happen, it is important for each player to accomplish three simple goals within this formation in the following order:

1. Hit the ball low.
2. Close the net.
3. Put the ball away.

For this chapter, we will not break down each individual player's responsibilities because they are all so similar. However, I will point out that if you find yourself at the baseline and the other three players are at the net positioned where they should be (as explained in Chapter 2) and you want to approach the net, it is absolutely necessary for you to hit your approach shot low over the net. In most cases, the approach shot should be hit crosscourt and down at the opponent's feet. As soon as the approach shot is hit and Player D comes in as the last of the four players to be in at the net, all four players now have a green light to move forward. It is not necessary to bother covering the lob here if you follow the order of the goals listed above—hit the ball low and then close the net. To be more specific, hit the ball low and try to get as close to the net as possible before your opponent hits the ball. This is a very limited window of time, so make your movement count by being explosive as you move forward. Just be sure to stop when your opponent makes contact with the ball by using the split step. If you hit the ball low and then simply sprint forward without stopping, there is a good chance you won't have time to react to the next ball. You may even get hit because you can't get out of the way of the ball.

In addition, make sure you carefully select when to hit the volley hard and when you hit it soft. An effective way to know when a hard or soft volley is appropriate is by recognizing the height of your contact point. If you are making contact with a volley above the net, hit it firm and with good form (Please don't swing at your volleys!). If you are making contact below net level, hit it soft. Hitting a low volley hard means your margin of error is low. It also means that your opponent will more than likely make contact with their next volley above net level in an offensive position. By making your opponent hit a low volley, it will be difficult for them to successfully lob it back over you. When they volley it back, you and your partner should be close to the net ready to put the ball away.

The last element I would like to cover here involves something I call the "toe line." The toe line is an imaginary lateral line that runs directly over your opponents' toes *(Diagram 15)*. As you can see from the diagram, there are two toe lines because you have two opponents. Targeting the toe line can be extremely useful in determining where to place your volleys, whether you hit them hard or soft. Hitting to your opponent's feet is commonly known as a smart target. However, if you can place your volleys anywhere along their toe line, you can achieve the same success because the ball is landing to the same depth as their feet. This makes for a very difficult volley for them and gives you more options when selecting a target.

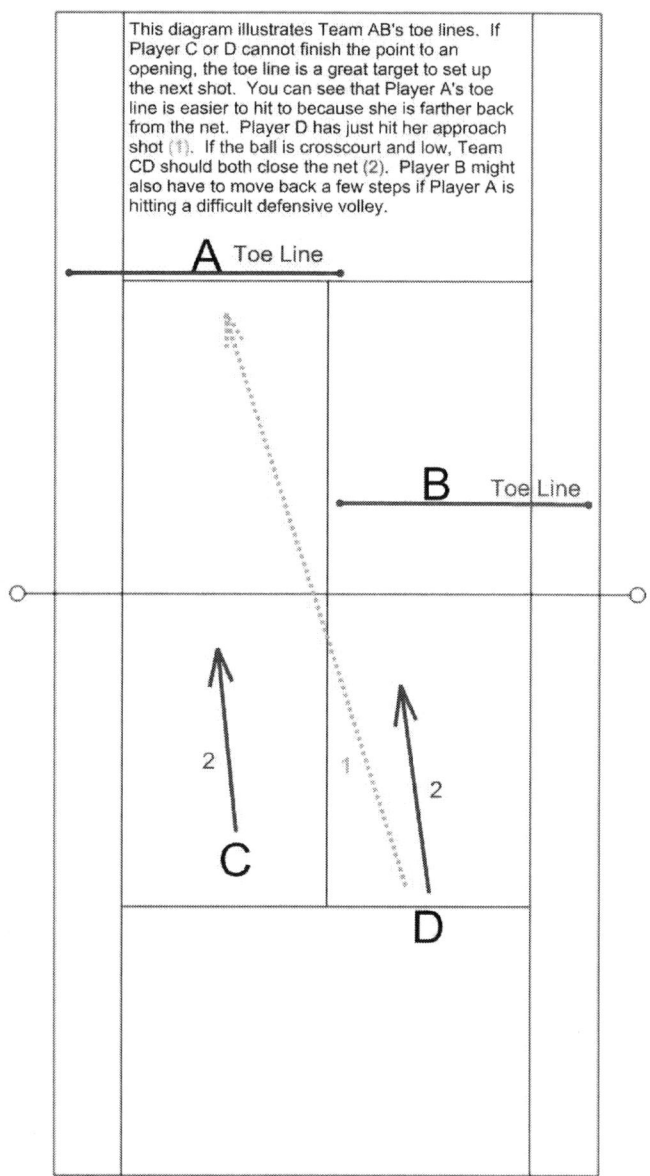

This diagram illustrates Team AB's toe lines. If Player C or D cannot finish the point to an opening, the toe line is a great target to set up the next shot. You can see that Player A's toe line is easier to hit to because she is farther back from the net. Player D has just hit her approach shot (1). If the ball is crosscourt and low, Team CD should both close the net (2). Player B might also have to move back a few steps if Player A is hitting a difficult defensive volley.

A Toe Line

B Toe Line

2

2

C

D

Diagram 15

To recap, all players should:

- Hit the volley low.
- Close the net.
- Put the ball away.

Drills for Practice

There are two drills that I like to use to practice this formation. The first one has all four players at the net starting from the service line. The ball is fed crosscourt and low by one of the two players positioned at the service line. The point is then played out from there as each team tries to hit their volleys low and close the net. Players alternate feeding the ball in for either a specified period of time or in a competitive format by keeping score. This is a simple drill, but very effective and fun. As a twist, you can play one game where lobs aren't allowed. This really gets players crashing the net. Then, allow lobs in the second game.

The second drill I like to use for this formation is a variation of the first drill. This time, one team is staggered to the deuce court and the other team has one player up and one player back (Chapter 2). The net player at the service line feeds a low short ball to the baseliner. The baseliner approaches the net and the point is played out from there with all four players trying to hit the ball low and then close the net. The players should rotate around so everyone gets an opportunity to practice approaching the net from both the deuce and ad court. The baseliner approaching the net should focus on closing the net as quickly as possible after the approach shot and using the split step when their opponent hits the ball, rather than stopping at the service line. Remember, the approach shot is the last groundstroke to be hit, which means all four players are now at the net. As a result, the need to stop at the service line is now gone.

What to Watch for: 4.0 and Above

As the level of play increases, each player's proper utilization of time becomes paramount. And, this formation presents the smallest amount of time on the tennis court because all 4 players are so close to the net. A point can become extremely fast as rapid-fire volleys are exchanged. What is important to remember is that many times it is better to take pace off the ball in close quarters. By hitting the ball low over the net and softer toward your opponent's toe line, you give yourself more time to close the net while also making them hit a difficult volley. It is also important to note that if you make the mistake of hitting your volley soft and well short of the toe line, higher-level players will let the ball bounce and hit an offensive reply (topspin groundstroke, lob, slice low to your toe line, etc.). The best way to succeed from this formation at higher levels is to vary your pace. Avoid becoming predictable by hitting only hard volleys. Practice using soft volleys to the toe line as well as firm volleys and follow up those volleys with explosive movement forward toward the net.

What to Watch for: 3.5 and Below

In my experience, most players at this level play within this formation one of two ways:

1. *They are fearless and move really close to the net.*
2. *They rarely move off the service line.*

Both types of players tend to play in one of these two ways regardless of where their own volley goes. If you are fearless in closing the net, make sure you also remain accurate and hit the appropriate volley (hard, soft, toe line, etc.) to maximize your fearless net positioning. If you don't like moving close to the net from this formation, start by practicing your volley quality. Can you keep the ball low over the net? Can you hit soft or hard volleys when appropriate? Can you target the toe line? Once your confidence rises in executing the appropriate volley, start inching your way closer to the net behind each volley. You might surprise yourself how effective you can be when up close to the net after executing an effective set-up volley.

SPECIALTY FORMATIONS

After covering the three most common formations you will use and see on the doubles court, it is important to now cover some lesser-known formations.

Some of these formations happen due to circumstances that take place throughout a point, while others are strategically planned before the point begins. In either case, it is important to understand each formation, know where to position yourself and your shots.

Chapter 4

1-Up, 1-Back,
Down-the-Line from Each Other

General Overview

This formation happens more than the average player might think, especially in matches where lobs are a common shot. As discussed in Chapter 1, most points begin within the 1-up, 1-back on both sides formation. If Player A hits a lob down-the-line over Player C and Player D runs behind the baseline to get it off the bounce *(Diagram 12)*, the new formation consists of net players and baseliners down-the-line from each other *(Diagram 16)*. At this point, Player D has several options from which to choose. However, in keeping to the Set-up Player and Finisher mindset established earlier in the book, let's discuss the option that best adheres to that formational truth. For educational purposes, we are going to assume that Player D is able to get to the ball in time to hit it under control.

Player A

When Player A lobs down-the-line over Player C, she should immediately look to see if the lob will successfully go over Player C's head and whether or not Player D is going to hit it out of the air or let it bounce. As soon as Player A knows that the lob is going to bounce, she should run forward. How far? Since Player A is down-the-line from the ball, that makes them the Finisher. As a result, Player A can run as far forward as they can get before stopping with a well-timed split step. At the same time, Player B should be back at the service line *(Diagram 17)*. This is the fundamental play that will ensure that Team AB is keeping to their staggered formation.

As Team AB becomes more familiar with the formations outlined in this book and are able to find positional chemistry, it will be much easier to see patterns and make adjustments as necessary. For example, in this situation the most likely shot hit back by Player D is a lob. Team AB might be aware of this and as a result, Player A stops at the service line to prepare for an overhead *(Diagram 18)*.

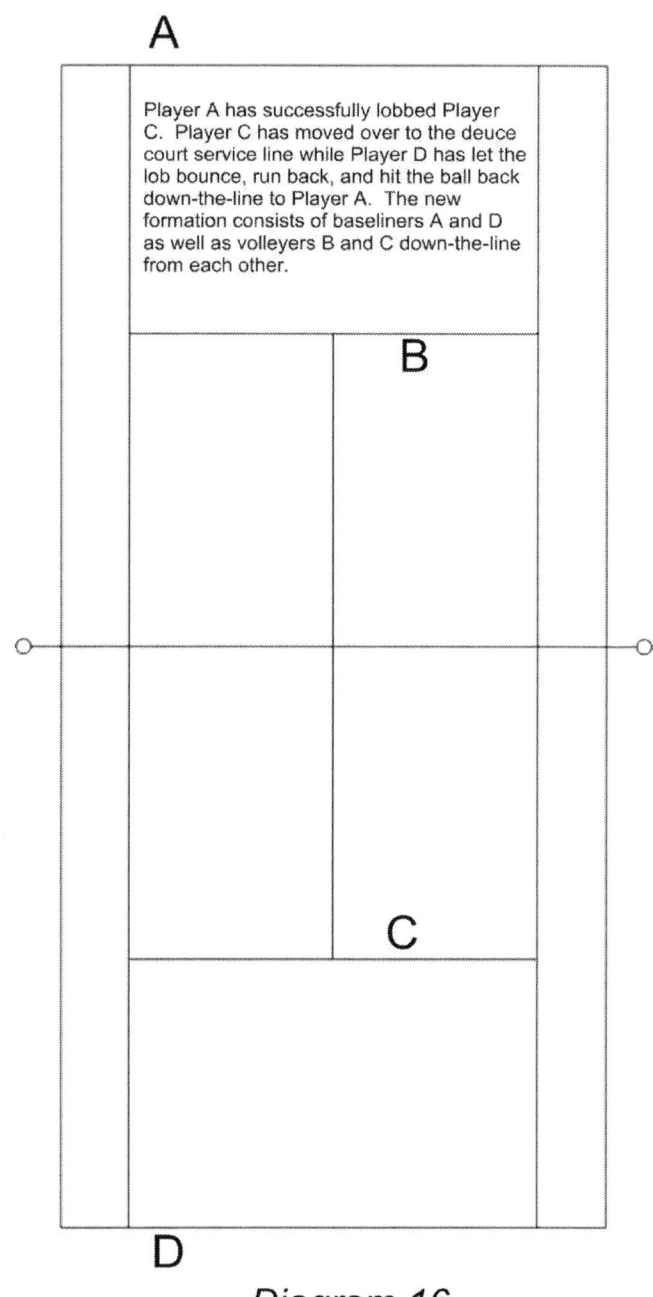

A

Player A has successfully lobbed Player C. Player C has moved over to the deuce court service line while Player D has let the lob bounce, run back, and hit the ball back down-the-line to Player A. The new formation consists of baseliners A and D as well as volleyers B and C down-the-line from each other.

B

C

D

Diagram 16

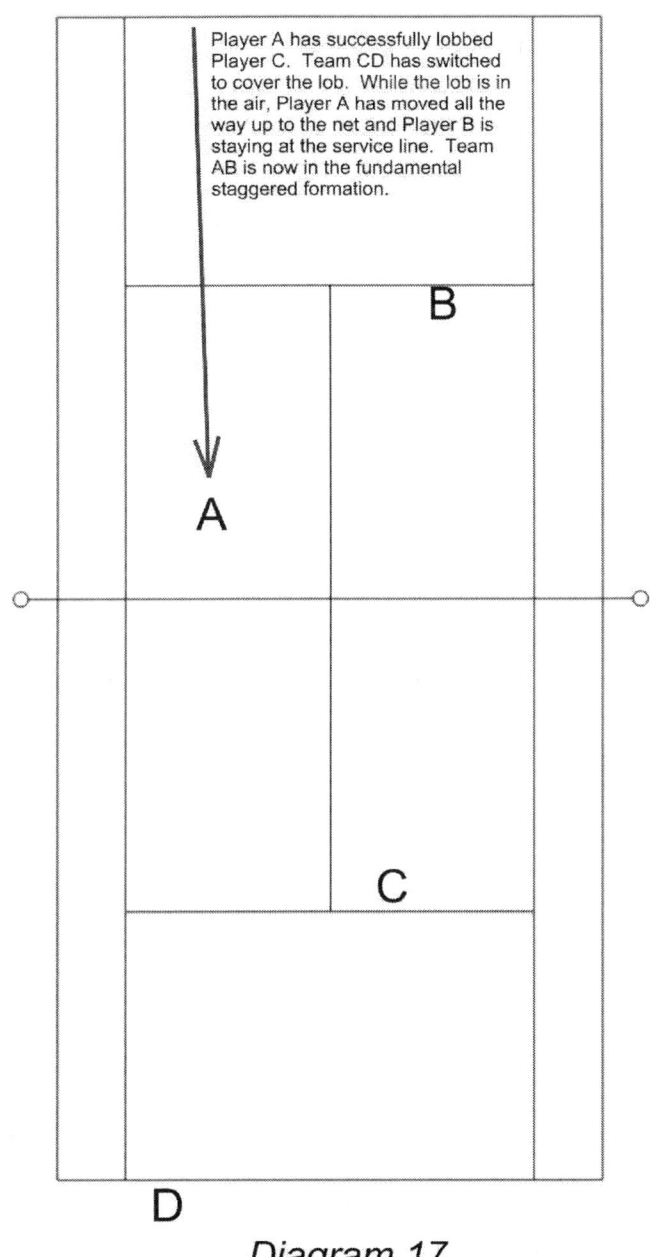

Player A has successfully lobbed Player C. Team CD has switched to cover the lob. While the lob is in the air, Player A has moved all the way up to the net and Player B is staying at the service line. Team AB is now in the fundamental staggered formation.

Diagram 17

As stated earlier, it is very important that fundamental positioning comes first followed by team adjustments. This means that Team AB should be in communication between points about the patterns each player sees and then make their team adjustment. Player A and B should not move around based on comfort zones or because of in-point individual adjustments, which will result in open gaps and uncertainty regarding coverage responsibilities. If done correctly in the situation above, Player B should be well aware that Player A is stopping at the service line as it happens because that pattern has already been discussed between points.

Player B

As Player A's lob successfully lands over Player C's head, it might be tempting for Player B to run forward in an attempt to put away a volley or short overhead. There are times when closing the net like this will work, but only if Player D does not or cannot effectively lob. Otherwise, Player B should only move forward if he believes Player D is not going to lob and if Player A stays back at the baseline *(Diagram 19)*. His fundamental position should first be at the service line so the lob can be covered and he can honor his position as the Set-up Player when Player A approaches the net *(Diagram 17)*. Making the adjustment to have Player B close the net should be because Team AB has seen this pattern and are both on the same page. If Player B randomly chooses to close the net and Player D lobs deep crosscourt, neither player on Team AB can cover it. Being crosscourt from the ball, what Player B should do is honor their responsibility as the Set-up Player and stay at the service line. As the lob carries over Player C's head, Player B needs to pay attention to where their partner is going. Is Player A moving to the service line and then stopping? If so, Player B should be prepared to hit any ball that comes their way and let Player A cover their half of the court, including lobs. On the other hand, is Player A moving as close to the net as possible to get into a finishing position? If that's the case, Player B needs to be prepared to cover the court as they would in Chapter 2—anything that comes crosscourt and all lobs.

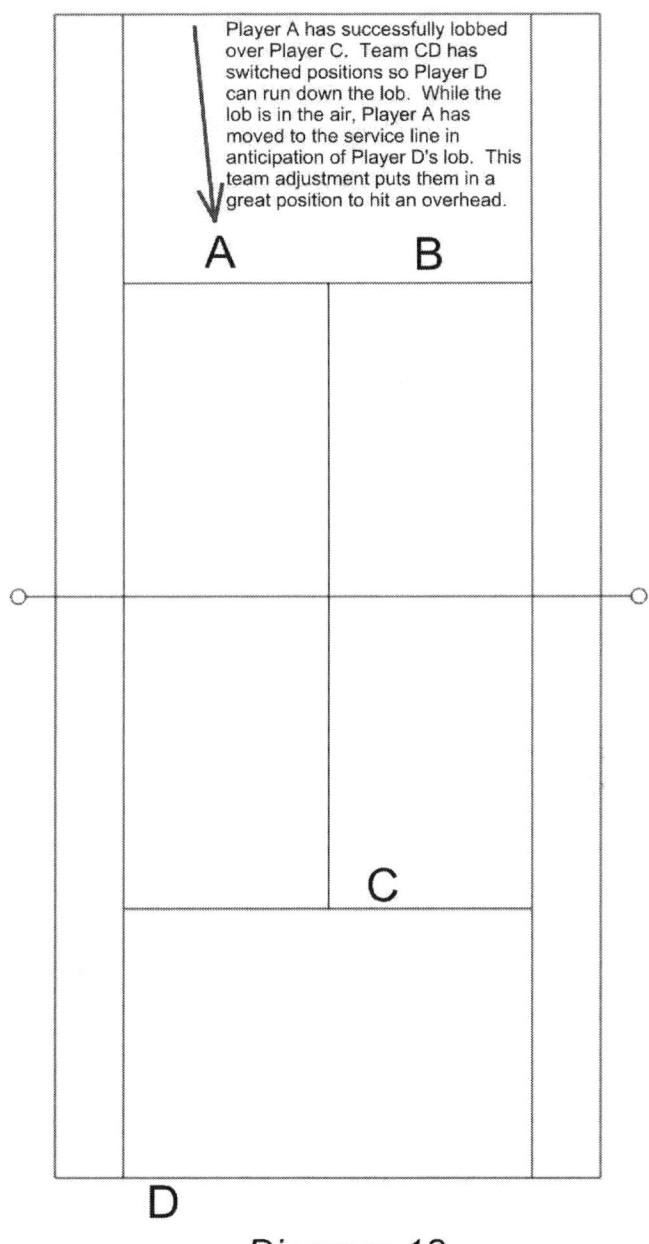

Player A has successfully lobbed over Player C. Team CD has switched positions so Player D can run down the lob. While the lob is in the air, Player A has moved to the service line in anticipation of Player D's lob. This team adjustment puts them in a great position to hit an overhead.

Diagram 18

A

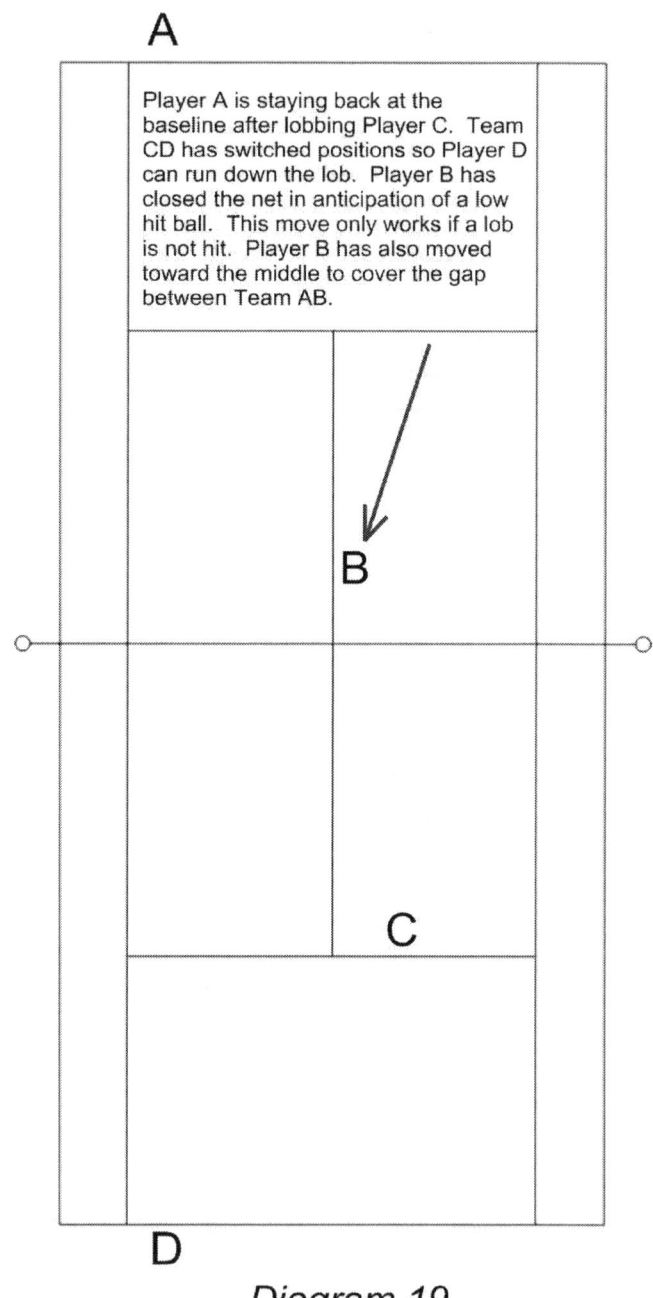

Player A is staying back at the baseline after lobbing Player C. Team CD has switched positions so Player D can run down the lob. Player B has closed the net in anticipation of a low hit ball. This move only works if a lob is not hit. Player B has also moved toward the middle to cover the gap between Team AB.

B

C

D

Diagram 19

Player C

As soon as Player C determines that Player A's lob is going over their head, Player C needs to move to the other half of the court and remain at the service line near the "T" *(Diagram 16)*. Player C also needs to look and see if Player A is staying at the baseline or moving forward to the net. From the service line, Player C is now prepared to defend as Player D hits the ball back. If Player D hits the ball low over the net, Player C should be ready to move forward and attack if either Player A or B floats a volley. If Player D lobs the ball back, it is a good idea for Player C to utilize the time the lob is in the air to move back to the baseline. It is very difficult to defend against an overhead from the service line, which makes retreating all the way to the baseline a smart move.

> *Side Note: It is important for Player C to move quickly to get back and then stop with a split step. Many times, players will try to retreat to the baseline only to find that they are still backpedaling as their opponent strikes the ball. Using a proper split step is important every time your opponent hits the ball, but it is extremely important from this defensive position.*

If Player D can lob the ball deep, then Team CD can now move into the fundamental staggered position or to the service line together in anticipation of a lob, depending on whichever team strategy they have decided to use *(Diagram 20)*.

Player D

As Player D sees the lob going over Player C's head, she should move over and decide which type of shot to hit back. Many players in this position will quickly decide to lob the ball back, which is the only option in many cases. For example, if Player A's lob is so good that it might bounce into the fence so high that Player D is just trying to reach it, lobbing the ball back in play is really the only shot to hit. However, if Player D has time to let the lob bounce up and then drive it back over the net, this gives Player C a chance to play aggressively at the net. Both lobbing the ball back and driving the ball can be good options. But, it is important that Player D is aware if Player A has run into the net or is staying back at the baseline. If Player A has come into the net, Player D should try to either:

- Lob the ball deep enough over either Player A or B's head that an overhead reply is not possible.

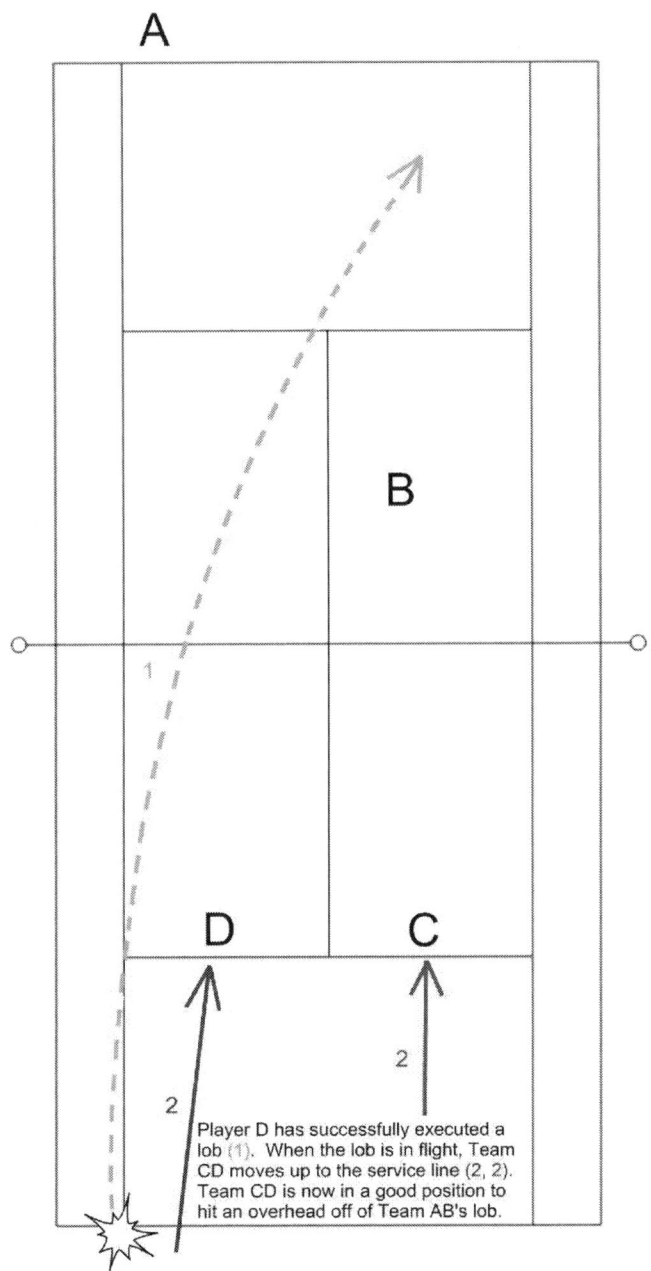

Player D has successfully executed a
lob (1). When the lob is in flight, Team
CD moves up to the service line (2, 2).
Team CD is now in a good position to
hit an overhead off of Team AB's lob.

Diagram 20

- Hit the ball low to either Player A or B's toe line (whoever is farthest back from the net).

If Player A has stayed at the baseline, Player D should try to either:

- Lob the ball deep down-the-line to Player A (or crosscourt if Player B is close to the net) and then run either close to the net in the fundamental staggered position or to the service line in anticipation of a lob reply.

- Drive the ball deep down-the-line to Player A. From here, if Player D prefers to hit groundstrokes, she can continue to hit from the baseline with Player A to set up Player C. If Player D prefers to play at the net, she can try to approach the net down-the-line to Player A. With each volley, Player D can continue to close the net as the Finisher. Player C would remain at the service line to maintain proper staggered positioning.

Side note: I would like to take a minute to explain what Player C and Player B should be doing if Players A and D are exchanging groundstrokes down-the-line rather than lobbing or trying to approach the net. Similar to Chapter 1, the two net players should move forward offensively toward the net and then retreat defensively toward the service line (Diagram 21). This is the rare instance that goes against the rule of Set-up Player and Finisher. The volleyers (crosscourt from the ball) move forward with the ball in an attempt to be offensive and put away a volley. The baseliners (down-the-line from the ball) try to hit an offensive shot to set up their partner. This is the opposite of how it is in every other formation. This trend continues as long as groundstrokes are hit back and forth down-the-line. If one team has seen a pattern of lobs from their opponent, then the net player can adjust and stay back at the service line, so they don't get lobbed. The difficulty for aggressive volleyers in this position is that it is hard to poach and get involved at the net because there is no crosscourt angle to cut off. If Team AB wants Player B to hit a finishing volley, Player A needs to try to place her groundstroke deep and as close to the middle as possible (Diagram 22). Player A does have to be accurate when aiming this way because if the ball travels too far crosscourt, Player D will have a chance to pick off a volley. If hit successfully away from Player D, Player C's reply will be from closer to the middle of the court, which will give Player B a better poaching opportunity.

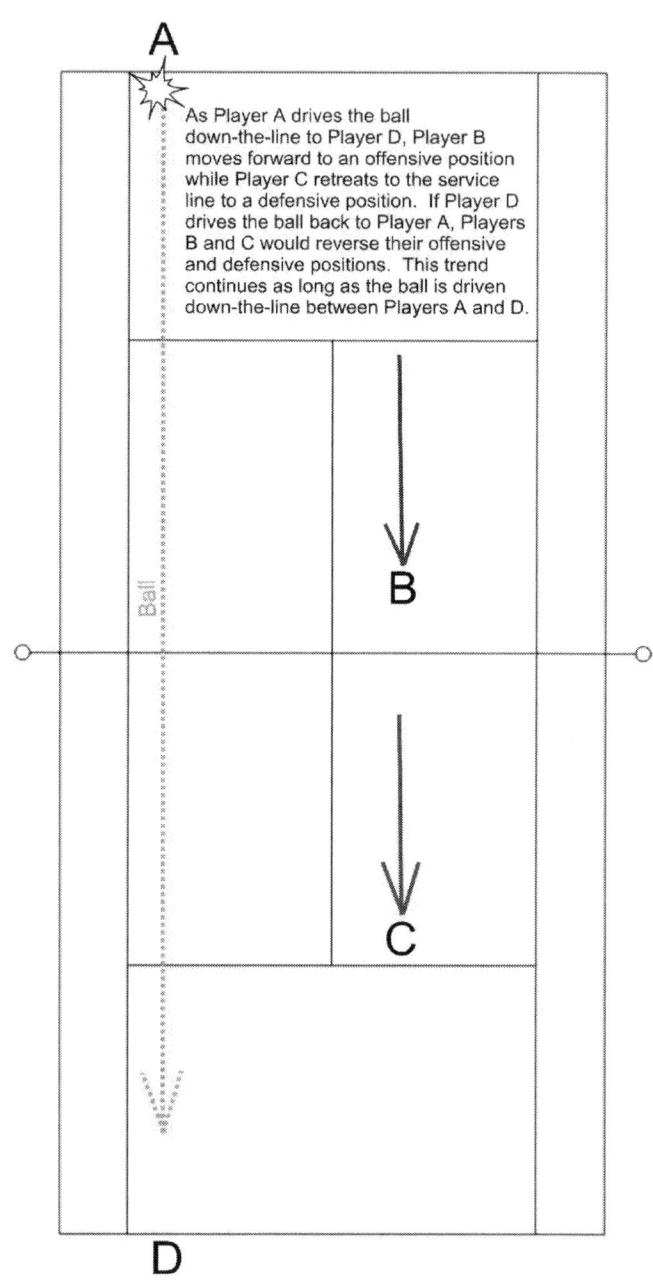

As Player A drives the ball down-the-line to Player D, Player B moves forward to an offensive position while Player C retreats to the service line to a defensive position. If Player D drives the ball back to Player A, Players B and C would reverse their offensive and defensive positions. This trend continues as long as the ball is driven down-the-line between Players A and D.

Diagram 21

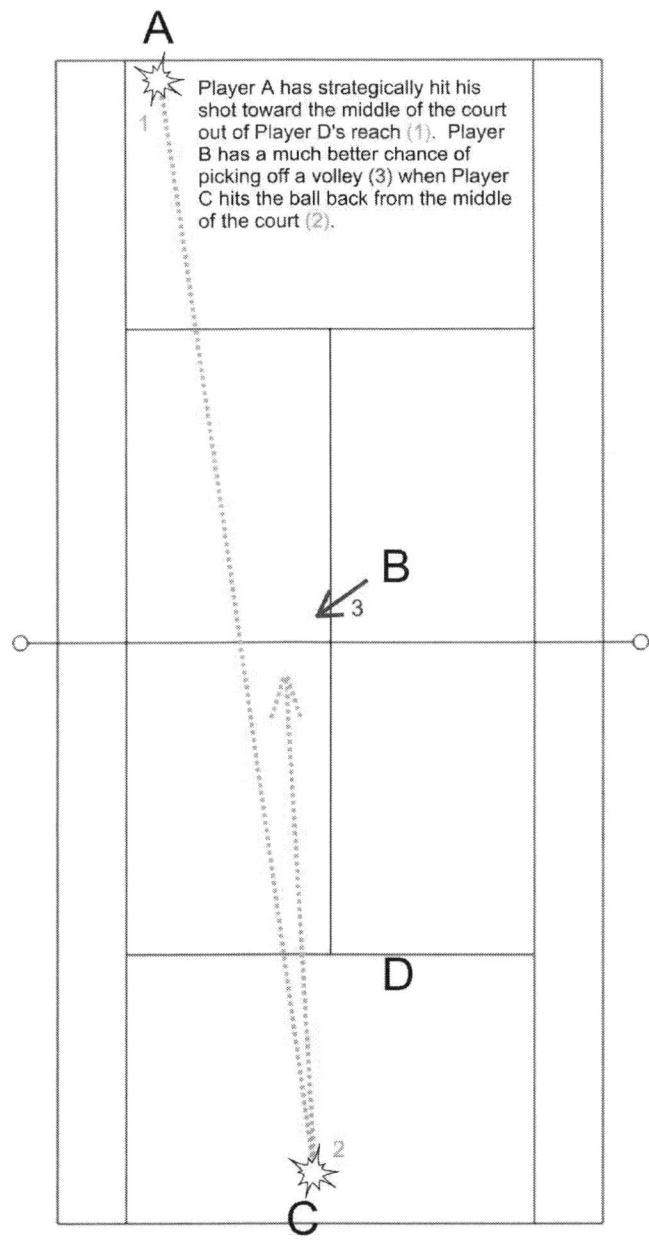

A

Player A has strategically hit his shot toward the middle of the court out of Player D's reach (1). Player B has a much better chance of picking off a volley (3) when Player C hits the ball back from the middle of the court (2).

B

D

C

Diagram 22

Drills for Practice

A very simple drill to practice this formation is to start with four players on the court in a 1-up, 1-back, crosscourt from each other formation as outlined in Chapter 1. One of the two baseline players feeds a lob down-the-line over the opposing net player. The point is played out from there. Baseliners can practice lobbing the ball back or driving the ball back. The baseliner that fed the original lob can practice staying back at the baseline and also running into the net. Partners really need to make sure they are in sync if the baseline player runs into the net because it is important that they are both able to make the transition from this formation into a traditional staggered net position. This requires excellent communication and an awareness of where the partner is positioned.

A variation of this formation is to start with all four players in 1-up, 1-back down-the-line from each other. The ball is fed from a baseliner down-the-line to the other baseliner and the point is played out from there. Baseliners can practice hitting their shots deep and as close to the middle as possible and volleyers can practice moving across to poach.

What to Watch for: 4.0 and Above

At higher levels of play, this formation is usually not sustained for very long because one of the two baseline players will find a way to get to the net. They may drive the ball deep down-the-line and run into the net. They may place their groundstroke down at the volleyer's feet and then come into the net. If the baseliner is forced to stay back at the baseline due to a high-quality shot from their opponent, that typically means that the opponent is coming into the net and the formation has now changed to a traditional one. In addition, if the baseline player is forced into a lobbing situation, most opponents will take the lob out of the air as either an overhead, high volley, or swinging volley because these shot options produce offense.

What to Watch for: 3.5 and Below

This formation tends to happen more often at lower levels as lobs are used more frequently. The typical pattern involves an exchange of lobs back and forth. One complaint I hear from some of my adult students is that lobbing the ball back and forth is boring and they're not sure how to avoid this scenario. If this happens, you should try to hit your lob as deep in the court as possible, pushing your opponent backward. While your lob is in flight, quickly identify if it will land deep in the court. If so, run up to the service line. From there, you can expect your opponent to lob the ball back. This should get you an overhead opportunity. This tactic gives you a goal with your lob and an offensive way to finish the point.

Chapter 5

Australian Formation

General Overview

The Australian Formation happens when the serving team decides to start the point in a different formation than the traditional 1-up, 1-back crosscourt from each other formation. In Diagram 23, Player A is the server and has moved from the traditional doubles serving position to the typical singles serving position. Player B has also moved from the ad court service box to the deuce court service box. Once the point begins, the most basic scenario regarding the serving team's position is for the server to hit the serve and then move from the deuce court over to the ad court, either along the baseline or into the service line *(Diagram 24)*. It is possible to have Player B poach immediately after the serve, which Team AB should discuss prior to the point *(Diagram 25)*. Let's first list the advantages of this formation and then break down each player's responsibilities.

Advantage #1

In many cases, players choose to play in the deuce or ad court based on their return of serve strength. Many deuce court players prefer to hit their forehand crosscourt and ad court players like to rip or slice their backhand return crosscourt, which is why they choose to return from that side. Advanced servers will mix up their targets and aim down the "T" as well as out wide to keep their opponents guessing. However, aiming at a smaller target is more difficult and can result in a lower first serve percentage, which allows the returner to be very aggressive on second serve returns. By using the Australian Formation, the crosscourt return has now been taken away and the returner is forced to hit their return to a less comfortable target, such as down-the-line or a lob.

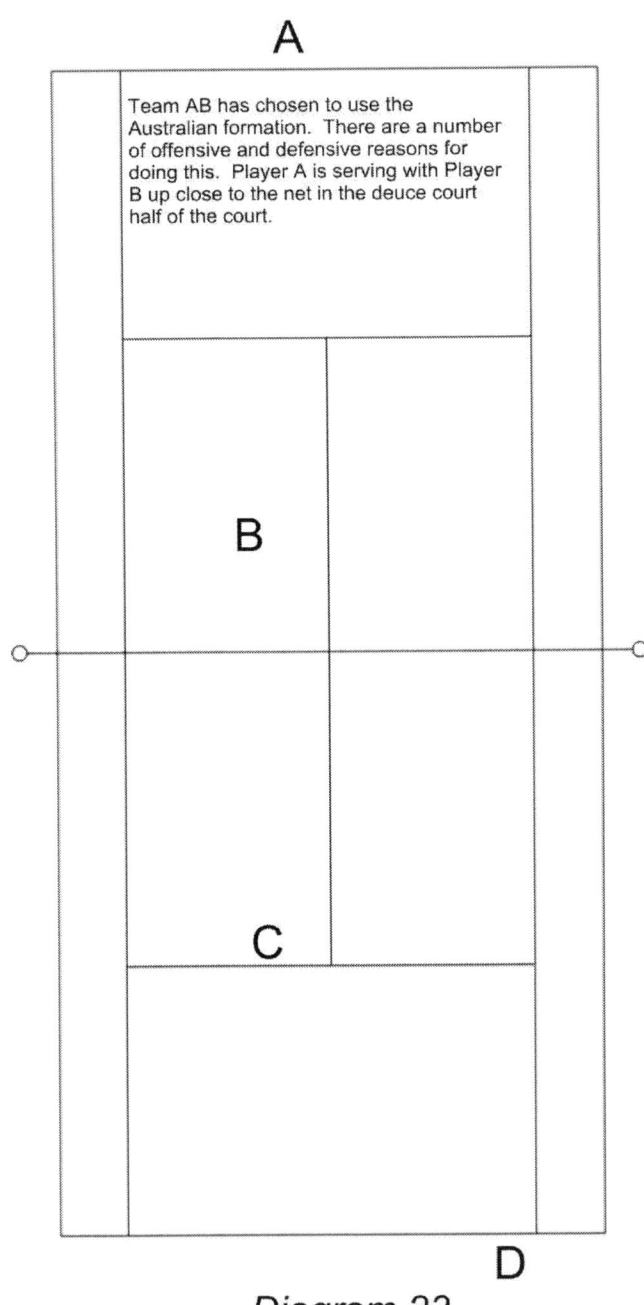

A

Team AB has chosen to use the Australian formation. There are a number of offensive and defensive reasons for doing this. Player A is serving with Player B up close to the net in the deuce court half of the court.

B

C

D

Diagram 23

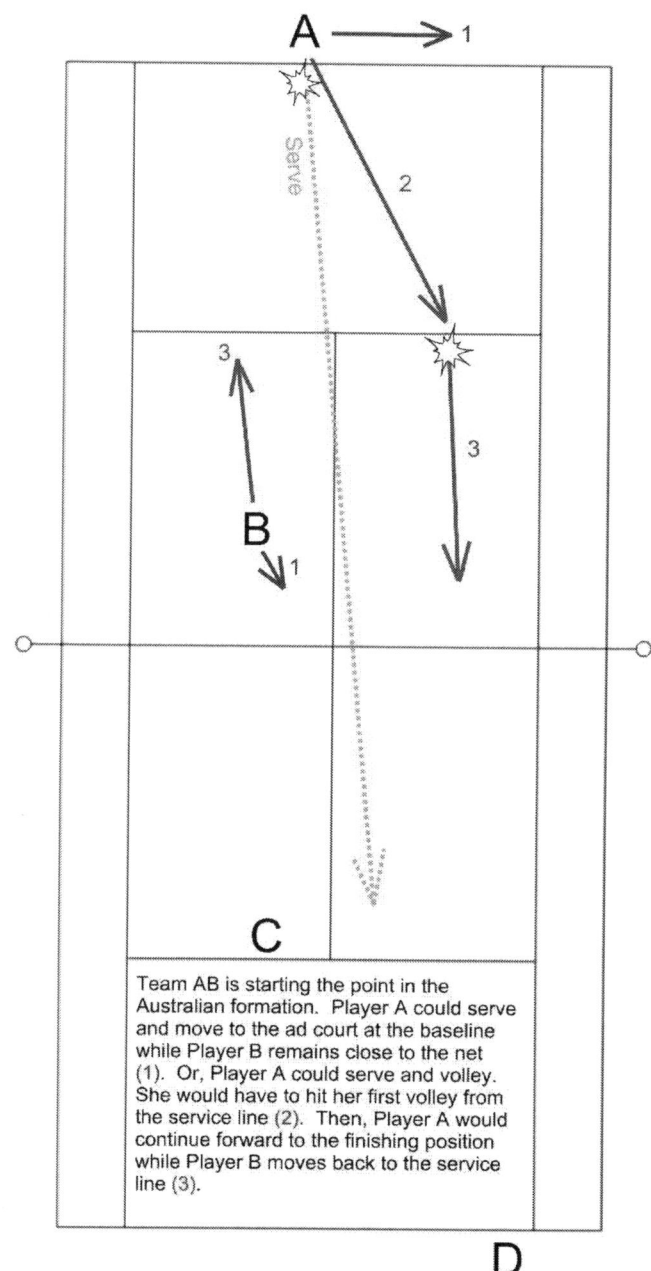

A ──────> 1

Serve

2

3

B

1

3

3

C

Team AB is starting the point in the
Australian formation. Player A could serve
and move to the ad court at the baseline
while Player B remains close to the net
(1). Or, Player A could serve and volley.
She would have to hit her first volley from
the service line (2). Then, Player A would
continue forward to the finishing position
while Player B moves back to the service
line (3).

D

Diagram 24

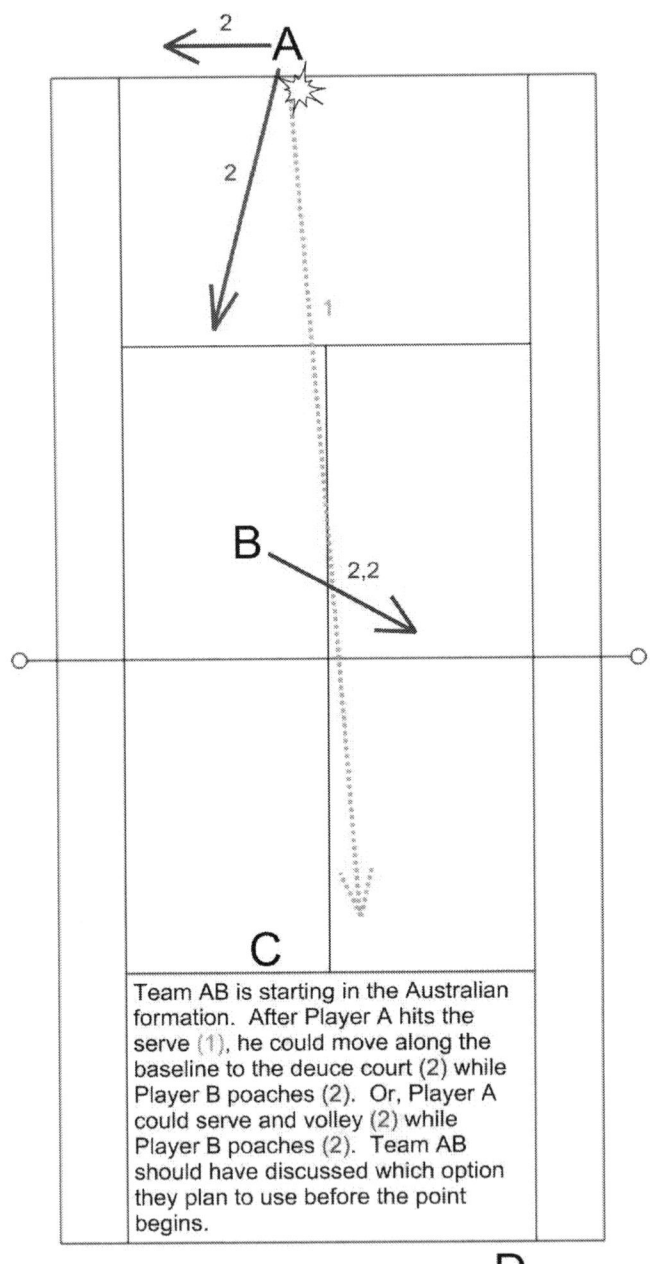

Team AB is starting in the Australian formation. After Player A hits the serve (1), he could move along the baseline to the deuce court (2) while Player B poaches (2). Or, Player A could serve and volley (2) while Player B poaches (2). Team AB should have discussed which option they plan to use before the point begins.

Diagram 25

Advantage #2

When starting in the traditional formation, I have had doubles teams ask me how to keep the ball away from an opposing net player who effectively smothers the net. Lobbing the ball can be an effective way to neutralize an opponent's aggressive position up close on the net, but it is not the best way to set up our partner and consistently generate offense for ourselves. The Australian Formation makes it easier to take an aggressive net player out of the point because the crosscourt angle has been taken away, which makes it very difficult for that net player to poach.

Advantage #3

Unless playing at a very high level, most players prefer either their forehand or backhand, both for groundstrokes and volleys. Using the Australian Formation allows you to use your strength of shot as often as you want. For example, let's say that a doubles team has two players that both love to hit forehand groundstrokes and forehand volleys. When one of these players serves from the deuce court, this doubles team is happy because they are both able to hit mostly forehands. However, when in the traditional formation in the ad court, they struggle as they both see more backhands. By utilizing the Australian Formation in the ad court only, both players can now position themselves to hit more forehands *(Diagram 26)*. From point to point, this team can play from a traditional formation in the deuce court and the Australian Formation in the ad court. This same thought process can be used in the reverse for players wanting more backhand groundstrokes and/or volleys.

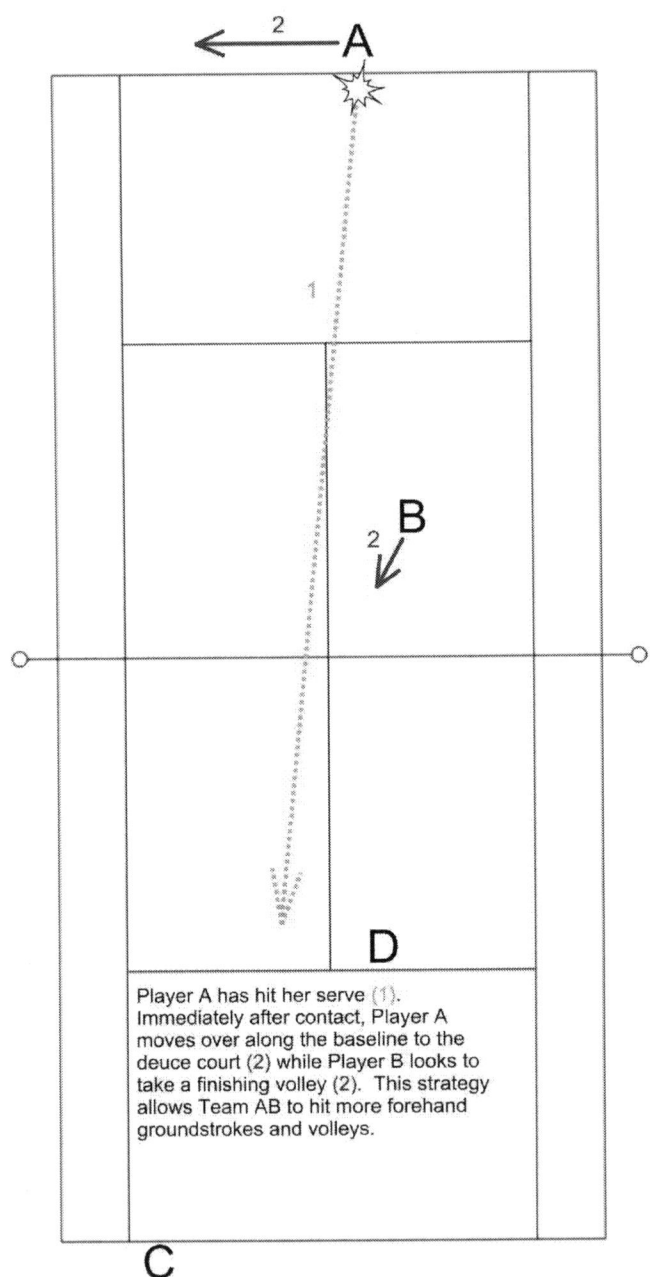

Player A has hit her serve (1). Immediately after contact, Player A moves over along the baseline to the deuce court (2) while Player B looks to take a finishing volley (2). This strategy allows Team AB to hit more forehand groundstrokes and volleys.

Diagram 26

Player A

Player A's first objective is to make a high percentage of first serves. When attempting the Australian Formation and the first serve is missed, I recommend going back to the traditional formation on the second serve. This relieves any unnecessary pressure and gives Player A the best chance to make their second serve. With this in mind, it becomes imperative that the first serve is made or else the formation can't be used.

Player A's next objective is to try to place the serve either down the "T" or out wide.

Side Note: "Where are you aiming this serve?" "I'm just trying to get it in." I have had this verbal exchange with various adult students plenty of times over the years. Don't beat yourself up if you are unable to accurately aim your serve. But, try to start devoting practice time to serving at targets. It is one of the essential components to playing high-level doubles.

If placing the serve to a target is too difficult to make, aiming to the middle of the box is fine because it is better to make the serve and then utilize the Australian Formation rather than repeatedly miss the serve and go back to the traditional formation for the second serve. Whether the server is effectively aiming to a target or simply trying to get it in, both players need to quickly discuss the plan before the point begins to ensure they are on the same page. Once the serve is hit, Player A should move from the deuce court over to cover the ad court. Player B will remain on the deuce court side at the net. As discussed in the General Overview, Player A could move over along the baseline preparing to hit groundstrokes or move up to the service line, ready to volley. Since Team AB discussed the plan before the point began, Player B should know if Player A is staying at the baseline or coming into the net. If Team AB decides to have Player B poach, Player A would either stay back or move into the net in the deuce court. These different movement options keep returners guessing and out of rhythm, which can cause a good returner to uncharacteristically miss returns.

Player B

Player B's mindset within this formation is to disrupt the returner. Team AB should have discussed whether Player B will stay or poach. In either case, as the serve is hit, Player B should close the net to place pressure on the returner. How close? Remember when we went over Set-up Player and Finisher? Player A is the Set-up Player here and the quality of serve dictates whether Player B can finish. Player B should err on the side of being too close initially because that gives him a better chance to finish and it puts added pressure on the returner. If the serve is too weak to generate a finishing opportunity or the returner is repeatedly lobbing, Player B might need to adjust and stay farther back. As always, Team AB should have ongoing communication about patterns of play and both players should be on the same page regarding any positional adjustments.

Player C

This position can feel odd (even claustrophobic) at first because the opposing net player is directly across from you. It is important that Player C stays at the service line near the "T" until the ball travels past Player B. Then, he can move forward to the proper finishing position or stay at the "T" if Player A decides to serve and volley.

This position can be a little tough to manage because of the uncertainty regarding Team AB's strategy. Are they staying or poaching? Is the server staying at the baseline or serving and volleying? Is my partner going to accidentally hit the return crosscourt, which will allow the net player to slam the ball at me? If Player D is struggling to get the return away from the net player, I recommend bringing Player C back to the baseline to take pressure off Player D's return *(Diagram 27)*. Once the return has been hit away from Player B, Team CD has the option to move forward into the net or stay back, depending on their strengths (volleys or groundstrokes) and team strategy.

Player D

When returning serve against the Australian Formation, it is important to not overthink the return and try to make it too good. It is easy to become distracted at your opponents' positioning and miss the return because you weren't focused enough on the ball. As the serve is hit, it is best to choose your target early, ignore your opponents, and hit the best shot possible. In most cases, deciding on a target and then changing your mind at the last second before hitting the ball will result in a missed or weak return. It is also ok here to lob the return back if the opposing net player is close to the net or if the serve is difficult to return. You might not generate much offense from this, but it can be a safe way to hit the return. Lastly, remember to call your partner back to the baseline if you feel too much pressure on your return.

A

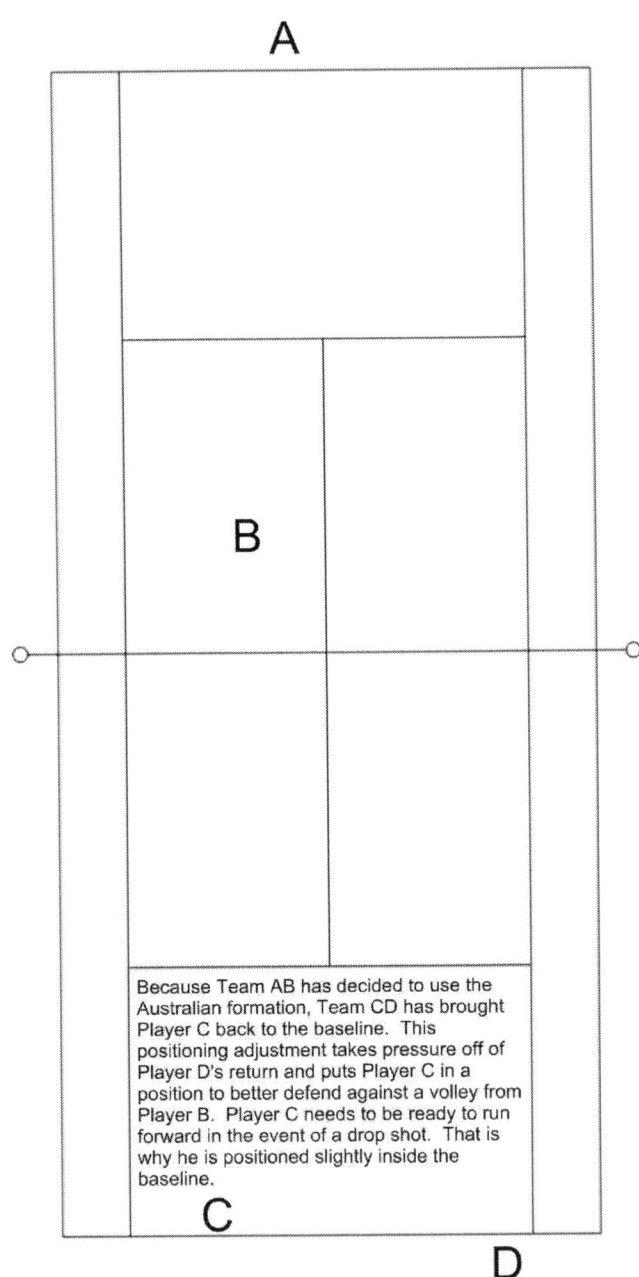

B

Because Team AB has decided to use the
Australian formation, Team CD has brought
Player C back to the baseline. This
positioning adjustment takes pressure off of
Player D's return and puts Player C in a
position to better defend against a volley from
Player B. Player C needs to be ready to run
forward in the event of a drop shot. That is
why he is positioned slightly inside the
baseline.

C

D

Diagram 27

Drills for Practice

In many cases, players that play doubles only practice serving from the traditional doubles position out near the alley. However, the Australian Formation positions the server near the center hash mark in the traditional singles position. At first glance, this might not seem like a big deal, but for those players that haven't played much singles, the angle difference may seem odd and require additional practice. I recommend that players practice serving from here because the entire formation is dependent on a well-placed first serve. I say first serve because I also recommend that if you miss your first serve, you and your partner move back to the traditional doubles formation for the second serve attempt. The reason for this is that there will inevitably be less offense produced from the second serve. As a result, this formation will not be as effective.

The best way to practice this formation is to simply try it. The best environment to try it is one where all four players are supportive and want to improve, rather than win. As you and your partner gain confidence, you can then use the Australian Formation in a competitive match based on a strategic need to use it.

What to Watch for: 4.0 and Above

As stated earlier, lobs are less frequent as the level of play increases. Serve speed also increases at higher levels of play. For this reason, the server's partner needs to be positioned very close to the net at the start of the point. The serving team also needs to decide on a serve target before the point begins. By knowing the serve target, the server's partner can plan ahead and close the net appropriately. If you are the returner and you are having trouble returning serve, have your partner start the point with you back by the baseline to take some pressure off your return.

What to Watch for: 3.5 and Below

At lower levels of play, one of the main benefits of using the Australian Formation is that it causes confusion. I had one of my adult students once tell me that she used the Australian Formation in a match only to have her opponent look across the net at her and say that it was against the rules to stand like that. This lady was

91

definitely confused. The typical shot selection when a player is confused is to lob. If you find that your opponents repeatedly lob the return, your serve is not generating enough offense. Generating offense should really be the primary basis of your positioning strategy. If the return is being lobbed, try to put more pace/spin on your serve, try to place your serve more accurately, try to take the lob out of the air as an overhead, position the server's partner slightly farther back to take away the lob, and so on. All of these produce offense.

Chapter 6

"I" Formation

General Overview

The "I" Formation and the Australian Formation are very similar in nature and are strategically used for the same basic reasons. The main difference between them is the starting position of the server's partner. Before the point begins, the server's partner will crouch down below net level along the center service line. In Diagram 28, Player B would crouch down so Player A could hit the serve without fear of hitting Player B with the ball. In addition, he should also be close to the net.

When looking at the diagram, you might first notice that Player B has to move somewhere following the serve, either left or right. As a result, it is necessary for Team AB to discuss the serve target and which direction Player B will move. This formation can cause great confusion for Player D because it is not clear if the return should be hit crosscourt or down-the-line. By not knowing where the serve is going AND where the net player is going, Player D can easily be indecisive or confused and miss the return. A smart play for Player D is to hit the return down the middle of the court. Because Player B will either move left or right following the serve, Player D should be able to drive a return down the middle. Player D can also bring Player C back to the baseline to take pressure off the return.

Drills for Practice and What to Watch For are the same as the Australian Formation. However, it is imperative when practicing this formation that the serving team talks about the serve target and which direction the server's partner will move following the serve. The last thing you want as the serving team is to have a miscommunication and leave one side of the court completely uncovered.

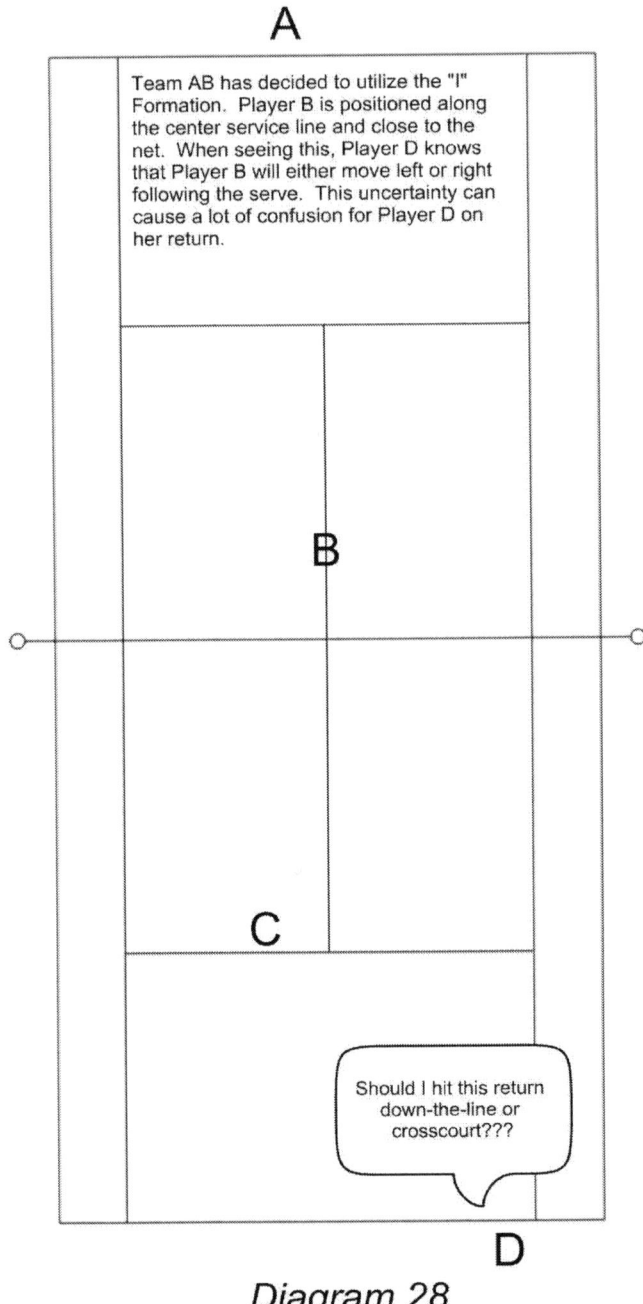

Diagram 28

Chapter 7

Both Back at the Baseline

General Overview

At first glance, it may seem like going both back at the baseline is a purely defensive strategy. It certainly can be used for that purpose, but it can also be used offensively depending on the strengths of your team.

The first question you may ask is, "What about the Set-up Player and Finisher? Does it still apply?" By starting both back, both players may end up being the Set-up Player or Finisher as the point unfolds. But as long as both players are back at the baseline, there really is no clear finishing presence because nobody is at the net. That doesn't mean two baseliners won't hit a finishing shot from the baseline (passing shot or lob) by exploiting openings/weaknesses shown by their opponents. The terminology just doesn't apply as explained earlier in the book. Where it does apply is if both baseline players hit groundstrokes that set up the type of traditional formation they are looking to move into, which would then bring Set-up and Finish back into the equation.

Let's discuss some reasons why a doubles team might go both back:

- When returning serve, the serve is so difficult to return that you are simply trying to get it back in play. Trying to hit the ball crosscourt to set up your partner is not even on your radar because returning the ball anywhere in the court is hard enough to execute. As a result, your partner helplessly feels like target practice for the server's partner. By bringing your partner back to the baseline, there is less pressure to keep the return away from the server's partner. It is important to initially defend and be scrappy enough to get everything back from the baseline, but try to quickly recover into a neutral position within the point and transition to the formation your team would like to use.

- You are again returning serve. The serve is not that difficult to return crosscourt, but the server's partner is an absolute rock star at the net. She is poaching and faking and has the wingspan of a condor. In this case, going both back will put less pressure on the returner. Try to hit the return anywhere around the net player and then transition into your ideal formation.

Years ago, I played a match against a team and one of the guys was 6'11" tall. He also moved well at the net. This team used a lot of "I" formation against us. We were either trying to return a 6'11" serve or trying to hit around a 6'11" net player when his partner was serving. Needless to say, we went both back a lot on our returns.

- The strength of your partner's game is the baseline. He can crush forehands and backhands, but feels uncomfortable at the net. When you return, you can bring your partner back to the baseline with you. After the return, you can go into the net and implement the 1-up, 1-back, down-the-line from each other formation. Or, you can stay back off your return as you both try to win the point from the baseline.

- You are serving. You love the net, but your partner is very uncomfortable at the net and doesn't like to volley. You bring your partner back to the baseline on your serve while you serve and volley. This is a very unconventional positioning strategy but fine to do if you are trying to maximize your strengths as a team and are on the same page when executing it. This puts you into the 1-up, 1-back, down-the-line from each other formation discussed in Chapter 4, which will best maximize your team's strengths.

Can you see how going both back can be done for offensive and defensive reasons? If you know your strengths and weaknesses as a team, you can formulate your formational strategy around your strengths. If it becomes necessary to adjust because your strength is not good enough to beat your opponent's strength, then adjust. Or, if your opponent has such a glaring weakness that making an adjustment would be smart, then adjust. But, start by building your strategy around your team's strengths.

Player A

When Player A steps up to serve in Diagram 29, the court looks very different because both the returner and returner's partner are back at the baseline. Without the threat of an opposing net player, it can be a real stress reliever for Player B. But, Team AB needs to determine quickly why Team CD is going both back. Is it for offensive or defensive reasons?

In addition, the court can look like there are so many targeting options that it is hard to determine which ones are the best. On a basic level, Team AB can hit to the weaker of the two baseliners. I have seen players hit their serve and then never realize that all of their subsequent shots are being hit to the stronger of the two baseliners. If Players C and D are both strong baseliners, then more strategy needs to be used. It is important to remember that even though Team CD is going both back, Team AB is still in a traditional formation. That means that Player A is still the Set-up Player and needs to primarily hit shots that set up Player B's finishing volley. Remembering this truth can really help reduce shot selection confusion for Team AB.

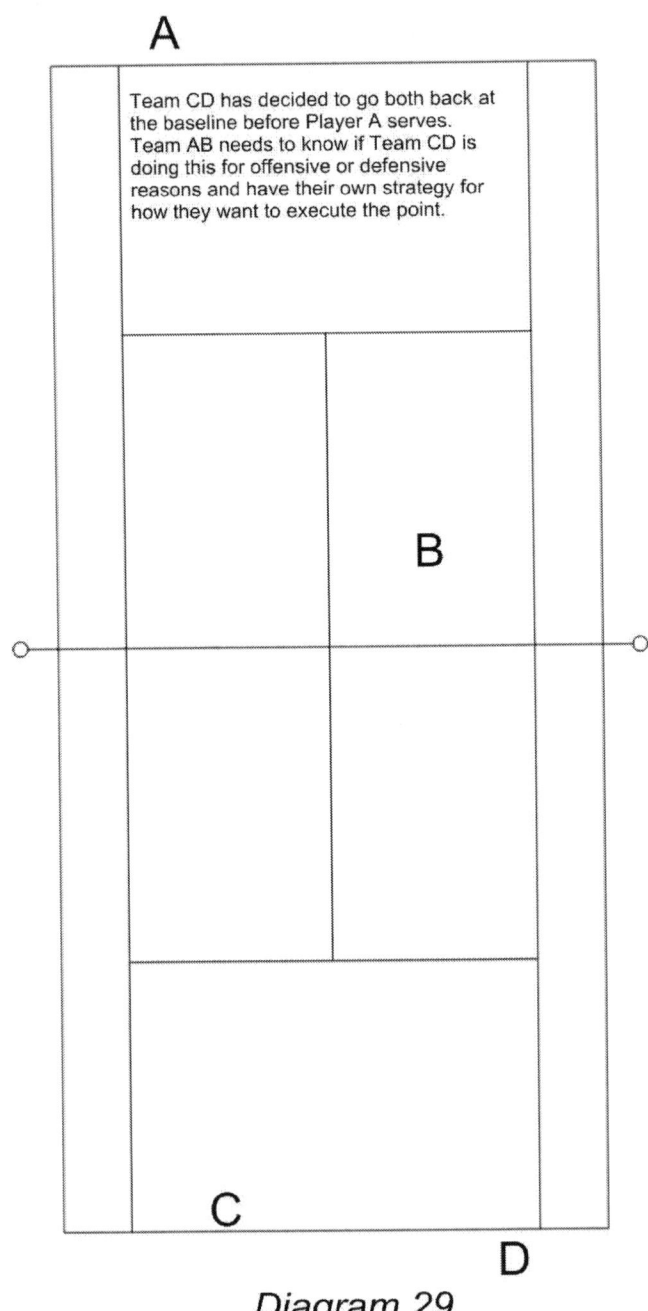

A

Team CD has decided to go both back at the baseline before Player A serves. Team AB needs to know if Team CD is doing this for offensive or defensive reasons and have their own strategy for how they want to execute the point.

B

C

D

Diagram 29

Let me run through a couple of examples to illustrate how Team AB can strategize against strong baseliners that are both back at the baseline:

- Player A is serving. Players C and D are quick around the court and have very good passing shots. The key here after the serve is for Team AB to take away Team CD's opportunities to utilize those shots. In Diagram 30, Player A has served and now is committed to hitting the ball consistently down the middle of the court. This takes away passing shot angles from Team CD and allows Player B to move toward the middle to look for a finishing volley. Without the threat of an opposing net player, hitting down the middle is safe for Player A and really sets up Player B to finish.

- Player A comes into the net after the serve to utilize her volley strength. Now within the both up staggered position, Player A takes the first available opportunity to volley the ball short, low, and through the middle. The middle takes away passing shot angles and hitting the ball short forces Team CD off the baseline. If executed well, Team CD should be scrambling to get up to the ball before it bounces twice. Even if hit back, Team AB should be in a great position to put away the next volley.

- Team CD is going both back so they can hit lob after lob. Player A can move in and stop just behind the service line while Player B retreats back to the same position. This is similar to

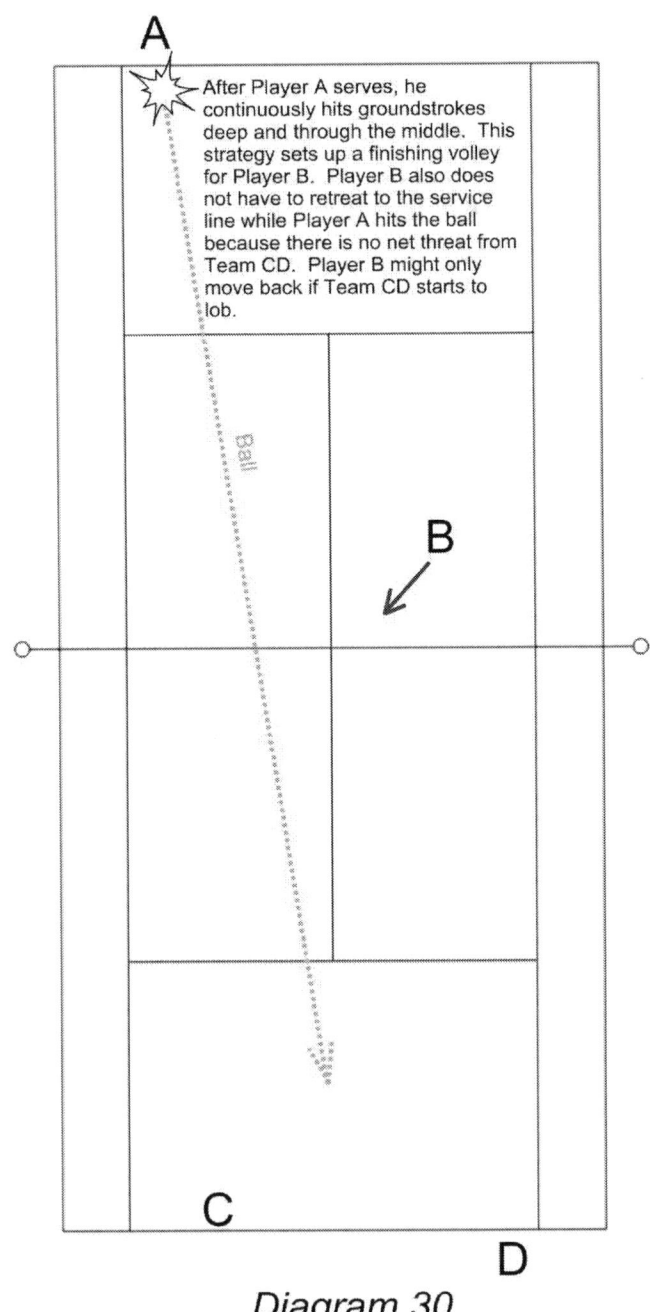

A

After Player A serves, he continuously hits groundstrokes deep and through the middle. This strategy sets up a finishing volley for Player B. Player B also does not have to retreat to the service line while Player A hits the ball because there is no net threat from Team CD. Player B might only move back if Team CD starts to lob.

Ball

B

C

D

Diagram 30

Diagram 18 in Chapter 4, except that Players C and D are both back at the baseline. Now, Team AB is in a good position to hit an overhead, which should be placed either down the middle to set up another finishing opportunity or hit off the court to end the point. If you struggle hitting overheads from this far back, then you now have another shot to practice!

Player B

Many times, this player can feel as though he is being taken out of the point. And if Player A doesn't hit good enough shots to set him up, this is exactly what can happen. What I mean is that Player B would love to put away a finishing volley, but the strong groundstrokes from Team CD are being kept out of Player B's reach, and he feels like a fish out of water. As a result, Player B can become increasingly impatient and try to poach on too many balls, wind up out of position, and get passed down-the-line. Player B needs to remember that he is still the Finishing player that needs to be set up by Player A. Until that happens, commit to proper positioning throughout the point and look to finish volleys at the right time.

Player B can be an asset even when not hitting the ball by faking (moving to the middle early as if poaching only to move back to the original position), which should draw Team CD's attention and make it more difficult for them to execute their groundstrokes. Also, without an opposing net player to provide a threat at net, Player B doesn't have to retreat to the service line when Player A is hitting from the baseline, as stated earlier in Chapter 1. Player B is free to stay up close to the net as long as he is not repeatedly getting lobbed.

What Team AB needs to realize here is that down the middle or crosscourt still are the best targets to provide Player B with a finishing volley. This is really important to understand because if Player A is at the baseline and randomly hits the ball down-the-line, there is a gap that Player C can exploit. It seems like the court is wide open and Team AB can hit anywhere safely, but shot selection still needs to be strategic to set up a finishing opportunity. For the most part, Player A should be going crosscourt or down the middle until he decides to come to the net. When he does come in, Team AB should make sure to stagger appropriately depending on the direction of the approach shot. When deciding which way to hit the approach shot, Player A needs to remember strengths and weaknesses. For example:

- Strengths: As a team, are we better staggered with Player A as the Set-up Player and Player B as the Finisher or vice versa?
- Weaknesses: Which player is weaker from the baseline, Player C or D?

Diagram 31 illustrates this concept very well. Player A is hitting an approach shot and wants to pick on Player C, the weaker of her opponents. Player A hits her approach shot down-the-line and closes to a finishing position while Player B stays at the service line in the setup position. From here, Team AB can consistently keep the ball to Player C until the finishing opportunity opens up. The bottom line is that Team AB needs to continue to honor their respective positions as Set-up and Finisher, hit shots that support those positions, and stay on the same page regarding any positioning adjustments that need to be made.

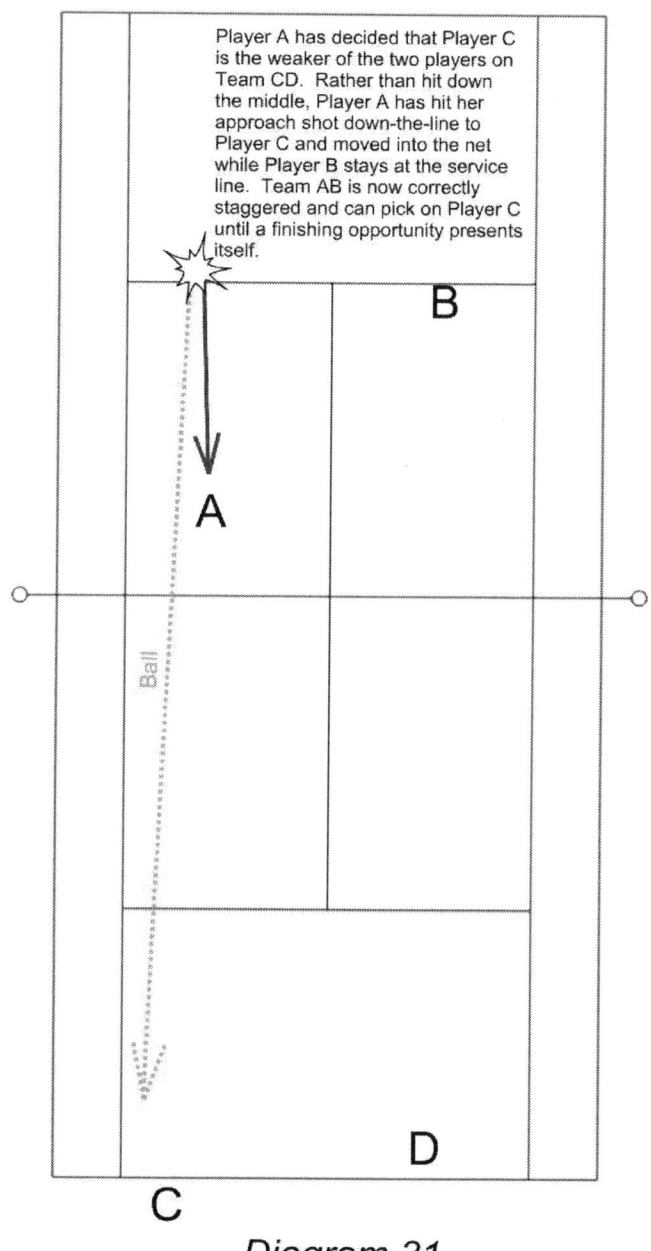

Player A has decided that Player C is the weaker of the two players on Team CD. Rather than hit down the middle, Player A has hit her approach shot down-the-line to Player C and moved into the net while Player B stays at the service line. Team AB is now correctly staggered and can pick on Player C until a finishing opportunity presents itself.

Diagram 31

Player C

Traditionally, Player C begins the point from the service line near the "T." But, going both back means that Player C now starts the point from the baseline. Team CD really needs to shift away from the initial Set-up and Finish mentality and instead try to use baseline groundstrokes to hit passing shots and lobs, generate errors from their opponent, or set up a short ball that allows them to finish the point outright or approach the net for a finishing volley. Team CD could be starting both back for defensive or offensive reasons. In either case, Team CD wants to play from their desired offensive formation as soon as possible. If they are initially both back for defensive reasons and would rather be in at the net, they should get one or both players into the net as soon as they have regained a neutral position within the point and the opportunity to approach the net presents itself. If they prefer to be at the baseline throughout the point, then they should be hitting their groundstrokes offensively to smart targets/openings—middle, down-the-line, lob, dipping at the net player's feet, etc.

Looking back at Diagram 27, you can see that Player C is at the baseline, but not behind it. It might seem odd for you to start the point inside the baseline in no-man's-land, but it is important to initially be closer because Player C needs to be prepared to run forward in case Team AB hits a drop shot or short ball. To effectively do this, Player C should try to anticipate the drop volley/shot before it happens. Here are a couple of indicators that a drop shot/volley is coming:

- *Team AB's backswing before hitting the ball*: If Player C can watch her opponent's backswing, that will clue her in on what type of ball is about to be hit. If the backswing is shorter than usual, something soft is going to be hit. If the backswing is taken back with an open racquet face, that lets Player C know that her opponent is about to hit backspin, which is what is used to hit drop shots and slices.

- *Team AB's position on the court when hitting the ball*: Generally, the farther back in the court Team AB is when hitting the ball, the less likely a drop shot will be attempted or effectively hit. For example, if Player A serves and backs up well behind the baseline to hit groundstrokes, she is probably not going to hit a drop shot from that far back. But, hit her a soft short ball and she may try to drop it.

After the return, Player C should be trying to either exploit the opening between Team AB or choose shots that take advantage of Team AB's positioning mistakes (Player B closes the net really tight giving Player C the option to lob crosscourt, etc.). By staying both back, this does make Team CD a counterpunching team. But, that does not mean that they are a defensive team. Counterpunching can be very offensive when groundstrokes are the strength of a doubles player/team.

Player D

With Player C now back at the baseline to start the point, Player D should feel less pressure returning serve. If Player B cuts off the return of serve with a volley, Team CD still has a chance to retrieve the next shot from the baseline and stay in the point. Player D's primary job here is to exploit Team AB's positioning mistakes, but also to initially keep the ball away from Player B with the return. After that, Team CD should work together to find openings and play the point they want to play. If Player A comes into the net, a simple strategy Team CD can use is to recognize which opposing net player is farther off the net and repeatedly dip the ball at that player's feet until a finishing opportunity presents itself.

The strategy of going both back is not overly complicated, but it is critical to understand that this strategy is very reactionary. You are taking what your opponent is giving you with their shots and positioning, and you are countering with shots that exploit weaknesses and openings. Where many players run into trouble is they try to hit their shots too offensively and end up making errors. When going both back, unforced errors are your worst enemy. Look for openings and choose high-percentage shots and you will have better success with this formation.

Drills for Practice

One great drill you can use to practice this concept is to put one doubles team in a 1-up, 1-back position while the other team goes both back at the baseline. The ball is fed to the returner (Player D) and the point is played out from there. This is great practice for all four players because points will typically be longer without serves and returns. In addition, Player B can work on her positioning because she doesn't need to retreat to the service line without a net player that would ordinarily pose a threat.

Another variation of the previous drill is to take the team starting 1-up, 1-back and bring them both up to the net. Both net players start at the service line and the ball is fed. The value of doing the drill this way is the net team needs to stagger immediately after hitting their first volley. As points progress, the net team will need to maintain proper staggered position, which can be difficult at times with their opponents both back. Scrambling to recover becomes important, along with clear communication between partners. The team at the baseline is trying to see positioning mistakes, exploit openings, and/or work their way into the net throughout the point.

What to Watch for: 4.0 and Above

At higher levels of play, teams that go both back are usually very observant when it comes to exploitable openings. They can see openings that are very slight and can accurately hit their shots to those openings. For this reason, it is critical that the team with one or both players at the net execute decisive volleys and position themselves correctly throughout a point.

One other noticeable truth about high-level play (especially in the both back scenario) is that baseliners with attackable opportunities will often hit the ball extremely hard right at their opponent. As I stated in Chapter 3, hitting the ball at your opponent is a legitimate part of tennis. It has always amazed me that in some tennis communities it is considered bad etiquette to hit the ball at your opponent. Many players actually make errors trying to avoid hitting the ball anywhere near them. Please realize that if you have a sitter and could easily hit the ball to a wide open court, but choose to crush the ball right at your opponent, that would be wrong. Or, if you're playing in a more social group and you decide to rifle the ball at the elderly player across the net from you, that would be very bad judgment. What I am describing are competitive matches where your high-level opponents cover the net extremely well, leave no openings to exploit, and you are in a position where the high-percentage play is to hit the ball hard right at them. There is absolutely NOTHING wrong with choosing that route. In fact, if you are playing a good team, they will have no problem with it because they also understand that hitting the ball at an opponent is part of the game. Keep your racquet up because they will probably hit it at you as well if they think it will win the point!

What to Watch for: 3.5 and Below

It is common to see players at this level go both back and begin lobbing repeatedly. If you are playing against a team that continues to do this, you are going to have to be patient. Strategically, the net player(s) should stay near the service line. Closing the net will only result in a lob going over your head, which will cause your partner to run over to hit it back. Your team will eventually tire out running down lobs while your opponents stand and watch.

If you are the ones going both back and lobbing, make sure you formulate a plan as to how you are going to win points. You could, for example, hit a lob and then both you and your partner move just behind the service line to take the replied lob out of the air as an overhead. Or, you could let their lob bounce and then hit a baseline overhead, which can be more difficult to lob back. The bottom line is that it is helpful to think of the last shot within your strategy being a winner hit by you or your partner. Many players over-strategize around making their opponents lose points, instead of thinking about how they want to win points. If your opponents make unforced errors along the way, that's simply a bonus.

SECTION 1

FINAL THOUGHTS

I hope you are starting to see why it is important to treat this book as a textbook. Feeling overwhelmed? If you just read Section 1 for the first time all the way through, it is understandable that you would feel that way. You might be familiar with most or all the formations, but needed clarification on specific details. Or, this might all be new, and you are discovering that there is much more to doubles than you thought. In either case, I hope you have more of a comprehensive grasp of team positioning and formations. Now, take each chapter one at a time, study, and practice. Ingrain it in your play so it becomes programmed. Once you do, then patterns of play will be easier to see, and the need to make team adjustments will become clear. Unsure as to what kinds of adjustments you may need to make? Let me give you a few examples of the many patterns you may notice:

- One of your opponents is noticeably weaker than the other. As a result, your team may choose to hit a few more down-the-line shots to pick on the weaker player.

- Your opponent(s) starts lobbing a lot of groundstrokes. As a result, the Finisher might not close the net as tight from the 1-up, 1-back formation or when both you and your partner are up at the net in a staggered formation.

- One or both of your opponents are closing in and are right on top of the net. Your team might choose to lob over them as it is too difficult to hit it to their toe line.

- As you come into the net, your opponent(s) backpedals to No-Man's Land (area of the court between the service line and the baseline…not a good place to stand on the court!). You may choose to hit your first volley down-the-line to exploit that player's bad positioning.

There are countless other examples of patterns that are recognizable and exploitable in any given match. The question is, can you see the pattern? In addition, how long does it take you to recognize that pattern and adjust? If you and your partner are committed to playing team doubles and can execute the formations discussed in this section, it will take you far less time to see the patterns. Executing these fundamental formations is step one. Communication then becomes critical so both partners are on the same page with any adjustments being made along the way.

It is also noteworthy that exploitable patterns are more difficult to recognize at higher levels of play. Better players just don't have as many weaknesses and tend to make better decisions. As you improve and play at higher levels, you will need to determine if an adjustment is actually needed or if the current formation/strategy simply needs to be executed better. There is a proper balance between strategy and execution that needs to be found for you to play smart and also play well. I have seen players and teams try to make so many adjustments within a match that they were never able to find any rhythm and ended up playing worse. In addition, be sure to make proactive strategic adjustments as often as possible for offensive reasons. Granted, there are times when you must adjust defensively because your opponent has a particular shot that you are trying to avoid or because they are so good you are simply trying to hang in there. Just be sure you are not always adjusting on a reactionary basis because that will allow your opponent to dictate play and stay one step ahead of you.

Time to get to work! Study this section again and practice the drills outlined at the end of each chapter with your partner. Begin practicing in a safe environment where winning is not the primary goal. Be willing to lose and feel out of sorts while trying to correctly execute each formation. There should be no fear of losing when practicing. It can be helpful to have four players on the court play out normal points but not keep score. One player can serve eight points, then the next, etc. This should hopefully remove fear from the equation. With no fear of losing, your improvement should be maximized. As you feel more confident with the formations, you can insert scoring back into your practices. It is important to put scoring back in play when you are ready because your team strategy should many times be dependent on the score. In addition, make sure that you evaluate points with your partner and put team positioning first. Remember, positioning is first, followed by targets, followed by strokes. Your team doubles will be much better if you operate off that priority list.

SECTION 2

TEAMWORK & CHEMISTRY

Now that we have a good understanding of team positioning and shot selection, we can spend some time going over team chemistry and some of the intangibles that allow a doubles team to play their best. Section 1 was mainly focused on proper team positioning as well as on shot selections that contribute to a particular formation's success. Much of the focus revolved around having a constant awareness of positioning and honoring your team's formation during points. In this section, I would like to put more emphasis on the in-between point time.

Some of you undoubtedly understand that tennis is a very mental and emotional sport. What is interesting about doubles is that partners have to work together to create the best team play possible. Each player has a responsibility to not only try to play their best, but also to bring the best out in their partner. You know you are on the right track when your partner's confidence grows when playing with you. In the end, if you and your partner can sustain emotional control, utilize the time in between points to plan/adjust your strategy, and build confidence in one another when facing adversity, you stand to play your best team doubles.

It never ceases to amaze me when I watch a doubles match and partners never say a word to each other. A point is played out, the baseliner walks up to the net, the net player walks back to the baseline, and the next point is played. It's almost as if they are each playing half-court singles…you cover your half and I'll cover mine. I like to compare this to other sports. And since doubles is a team sport, I like to make comparisons to team sports. Can you imagine what a football game would look like if teams never huddled up and a play was never called?

After reading Section 1, it should be obvious to you that communication is vital to a doubles team's success. However, effective communication does not just involve strategic evaluation and formational planning. It also involves working together to handle pressure, respond to adversity, capture and utilize momentum, and so on. These are just a few examples of the intangibles that make a doubles team great.

Chapter 8

Be the Ideal Partner

There have been countless times over the years where I have heard players blame their partner after a match ends. "My partner hit the wall," "My partner couldn't find the court," "My partner couldn't make a shot to save their life," and so on. Sometimes, they do it in a subtler way. They blame them but offer up an excuse for their bad play, "It was a bad matchup for him," "That just wasn't her kind of tennis," "He had just gotten back in town," "She has a lot going on right now," etc. In most cases, players don't blame their partner for an entire match, but for moments in a match or for a span of games. And most of the time, that span of games also happened to be the critical time when the match was ultimately lost. They can tell you fairly accurately when their partner played poorly. In all honesty, they may be right.

Obviously, both partners missed shots or needed to play better to win the match. The question isn't whether you or your partner played better or worse. That attitude certainly doesn't support team doubles. The real question is whether you helped your partner play better or made them play worse. Tennis is not about what happens in moments of adversity, it's about how you respond to that adversity.

Throughout the course of a doubles match, it is very common that one player plays well and the other struggles, only to have the roles reversed. This can happen multiple times in a match. If your partner is the one struggling, you can either help them feel relaxed and confident, or make them feel added pressure. At first glance, this may seem relatively easy. But, it really is a very delicate situation that requires a high level of emotional control. It's not just about using the right words and tone of voice, but also the right body language. Think that's a little much? Let me give you an example. If you double fault and see your partner's shoulders slump (even slightly) immediately after you miss your second serve, how do you feel? You might end up saying, "Sorry. My fault." The reality is that you should never feel the need to apologize to your partner during a match because you think you have let them down. Why? If you do, then you are no longer viewing the match from a team perspective, but from an individual one. If you double fault, so did your partner. If your partner misses an easy overhead, so did you. The score will always reflect this truth. If you do apologize simply as a courtesy, that's fine as long as you don't feel like—or, they don't make you feel like—you owe them one.

In terms of body language, work hard to carry yourself in a confident manner. You may be playing in a very important match or be playing against an amazing team, which makes you feel shaky on the inside. But, try hard to stand tall and display confident posture in between points. Not only will this help your overall confidence, it can add to your partner's confidence level.

In addition to body language, choosing the right words and tone of voice is very important, and it takes a tremendous amount of emotional control to do this well. Let's use the same example from earlier to illustrate what I mean. You are now the net player and your partner just double faulted. How do you feel? By the way, I forgot to mention that your partner just double faulted at 5-6 in the first set tie- breaker, which means your team just lost the first set. We all have different personalities, which means we all would respond to this example a little differently. Most players are either disappointed with their partner (self-focused) or concerned for their partner's feelings (partner-focused). Which category do you lean toward? Would your shoulders slump or would you want to tell them that everything is going to be okay? In this example, it is important that you approach your partner in the way that helps them recover quickly, even if that way is not your natural personality. You might be a helper by nature, which means you want to make them feel better. But to them, that might make them feel patronized when they just want to put it behind them and move on.

The way to find out how to best interact with your partner during difficult circumstances is to talk to them about it off the court. You will also learn how to best interact with your partner as you play more and more matches together. By doing so, neither you nor your partner will feel like they are stranded on their own emotional island. This teammate support should be an advantage of doubles. But if difficult circumstances are handled poorly by one or both players, it actually becomes a disadvantage. If you find yourself finishing doubles matches only to wish you had been playing singles, you might need to either look for a different partner or become a better one.

In addition to helping each other, each player also has a personal responsibility to keep themselves in check emotionally. If you tend to be an emotional person, this is going to be a challenging task for you. When unable to control your emotions, your partner will undoubtedly feel a heavy burden when playing with you. Let me give you an example:

Bob and Frank are doubles partners and Bob is quick to get down on himself and lose his temper. Frank now must try to pick up Bob and help him recover emotionally. If Frank is continuously having to do this, Frank now plays worse because he can't focus enough on his own play and gets no strategic communication from Bob. Since Frank's play got worse while trying to pick up Bob, what does Bob think after the match? "Frank couldn't find the court."

Let me give you one more example:

Bob and Frank are playing a match and Frank is a little off with his game. He's hit several double faults and is missing some routine volleys that he normally makes. Because Bob can't handle his emotions well, he begins stating the obvious. "Ok Frank, make your first serve here," "Need to get that volley over the net," etc. Consequently, Frank begins to get frustrated with Bob and thinks, "Thanks for the reminder. I was planning on missing my first serve until you said something." Not only is Frank dealing with his own bad play, he is also dealing with Bob's asinine comments. This only makes the task of playing better more difficult.

In the first example, Bob wouldn't even realize that his own poor temperament is the main reason Frank played badly. In the second example, Bob is doing a terrible job helping Frank play better. How could Bob not see this when it seems obvious to you and me? Bob's emotions are preventing him from thinking logically. Tennis players play their best when thinking logically. What do the pros look like in between points the vast majority of the time? Most of them look stoic, robotic, and extremely focused. This is emotional control at its best, and it's why they are professionals.

Many junior players lack the maturity to control their emotions and struggle with this concept. When in point situations on the practice court, I like to ask junior players to give me an evaluation of points when I can see they are losing their temper or getting upset. It's amazing how far off from the truth they are because they can't evaluate points logically while looking through an emotional cloud. When I ask them again later that day or the next day about it, they many times don't even remember what they said. When I remind them, they will chuckle at themselves or look a little embarrassed as to how absurd their thought process was, simply because they were allowing their emotions to take over.

The irony of tennis is that it is a very emotional sport that requires a tremendous amount of emotional control. You're not playing against a clock or a course, and you're not playing against a large team. You're playing against two people who may or may not display good sportsmanship or even play by the rules. This situation spikes the competitiveness within many people and can bring out a "win at all costs" mentality. Tennis is a sport that can cause successful, polished adults to behave like children...bickering with their opponents, throwing their racquet, swearing, name-calling, cheating, and so on. Make sure you are honest with yourself when it comes to your own emotions on the court. Talk with your partner so you can share the burden and work together when things get tough. As your ability to support your partner and think logically becomes more consistent, so will your game.

Side Note: If you are playing in a match where your opponent is clearly cheating (making bad line calls, for example) or using gamesmanship tactics, the best thing to do is to disengage from them as much as possible. You can question their bad line call in a calm, controlled manner. And if a tournament or league official is present during your match, you can go ask them to watch your match. But, don't engage in a verbal back-and-forth with your opponent. Your calm temperament will ensure that your opponent receives no added motivation and will require them to win on their tennis skill only. Typically, they're not just trying to win that particular point. They're also trying to get under your skin, so you play worse. An adjustment you can make is to compete harder, move quicker, and play with more energy. Show your opponent that their gamesmanship tactic will only spark you to put in more focused effort. Draw confidence from the fact that your opponent is searching for a way to win because they don't believe they can win on skill alone.

Also, you may find yourself playing a team, league, or tournament match with a multitude of spectators. If these people are cheering for your opponents, it can be difficult to ignore their potentially obnoxious behavior. But, that's exactly what you should do in this situation. Give them no reason to cheer louder or make crude comments toward you. This can be one of the biggest tests of your emotional control. But as already explained, emotional control is essential to your best play. Remind yourself that if you lose control of your emotions, you will probably lose the match. If you can do this while being heckled, you give yourself the best chance to play well, even in the midst of difficult circumstances.

Chapter 9

Process over Results

Anyone who has ever been involved in a competitive activity or sport has undoubtedly felt nervous. Most people are aware of what nerves are and how they feel, but it's important to understand why you might feel nervous in a tennis match. Simply put, you feel nervous because you care about the outcome. You have a strong enough desire to play your best and/or win the match that you begin to feel nervous. If viewed well and channeled correctly, nerves can be a positive thing and can provide you with an incredibly satisfying experience on the tennis court.

Anytime I talk to a player after a tennis match where nerves were present, the player is either emotionally high or low…more so than when the player wasn't nervous. And in my experience, players are more emotionally affected by how well they played in a tennis match as opposed to whether they won or lost. I can tell you that there have been many matches I have won where I didn't feel very good about the match itself, except for the fact that I found a way to win. Conversely, I have felt great about how I played in other matches, but still somewhat disappointed that I lost. I always cared about whether I won or lost, but the primary emotional feeling after a match revolved around how well I played.

If you feel unsure about this concept, think of it this way. If you play your best and lose the match, it is much easier to recognize how well your opponent must have played to beat you. As a result, the loss becomes acceptable. This means that your central focus needs to be on playing your best, not winning.

There are some important keys to handling nerves, both mentally and physically. First, let's go over what you might feel physically on the tennis court because of nerves:

- *Heavy:* Your feet might feel like they are in concrete and the racquet may feel like it weighs 50 lbs. As a result, you end up standing flat-footed during points.

- *Tight:* Long, fluid strokes begin to go away and get replaced with short, slow-moving swings that cause you to push the ball instead of hitting it.

- *Rushed:* Many players play too fast in between points when feeling nervous, which can make it hard to think clearly.

- *Winded:* When nerves set in, your heart beats faster and your breaths become shorter. This also burns more energy throughout a match, which can tire you out sooner.

Maybe you can relate to some or all of these feelings. If you remember back to any matches you played while feeling this way, it's probably not very comfortable. How do we overcome these feelings? There are several keys to overcoming the physical symptoms of nerves. If done consistently, you will find yourself playing well under difficult circumstances.

- Take your time in between points and control your breathing. Obviously, you can't take so much time in between points that you break the rules. However, you can be sure that you use the allowable time to slow your breathing and heart rate, which will relax your muscles.

- Put your racquet in your non-dominant hand. When nervous, it is easy to walk around squeezing the grip of your racquet tightly without even knowing it. Put your racquet in your non-dominant hand and relax your dominant hand in between points.

- Stay bouncy. Unless you are the server, bounce up and down on your feet just before the point begins. This will make you feel light on your feet to start the point.

- Immediately before the start of the next point, take a deep breath. The additional oxygen will temporarily calm your nerves and relax your muscles. This should allow you to execute a better serve or return.

Now that we've covered some of the physical symptoms, let's discuss nerves from a mental standpoint. Everything listed above that you might feel physically on the tennis court is the result of what you are thinking mentally.

Result-oriented thinking will undoubtedly produce an emotional response. "Ok. Make this first serve." *I feel nervous right now just writing that statement.*

Process-oriented thinking can prevent nerves and/or emotions from getting in the way of performance. "Hit the return crosscourt and move into the service line to the proper staggered position." *That thought brings together Sections 1 and 2 of this book.*

The result-oriented statement is focused on "making" the first serve, which is not always controllable. This uncertainty will cause nervous tension. The process-oriented statement is focused on "aiming" the return and moving to a particular spot on the court, which is completely controllable.

There are many catchphrases coined after process-oriented thinking, "It's not whether you win or lose, but how you play that counts." "Forget about winning and losing." The problem is that it is virtually impossible to simply forget about winning and losing. If you remove a thought from your mind, you must replace it with something else that will result in better play or else result-oriented thoughts will inevitably creep back into the picture. Process-oriented thoughts will result in better play, which will then contribute to more wins.

To start, program your mind to repeat the word "Process." Focusing on the process can mean everything covered in Section 1, it can be simple technical reminders that help you execute a given stroke(s), it can mean helping your partner in between points, etc. In short, it means focusing on your present play, not the future result. This can be very difficult to accomplish and is not an easy skill to master. But if done correctly, process-oriented thinking will help you play your best when you need it the most.

In order to become a process-oriented thinker, it is important to first acknowledge the fact that you feel nervous. Tell your partner as well. If you both have prepared for nerves, then you can help each other overcome them. Also, as difficult as this seems, you must learn how to embrace the tension. One way to look at nerves is to recognize that it is impossible for you to recreate this moment on the practice court. The confidence you will gain by performing well while nervous is substantially more than any confidence boost you can hope for in practice. In other words, you could hit hundreds of serves on the practice court and gain some degree of confidence. But, hit only one good serve when the stakes are high under nervous tension and your confidence will skyrocket. So when you feel nervous, enjoy the moment by positively telling yourself, "This is my opportunity."

Drills for Practice

One way you can try to create some nerves in practice is to put penalties on a lack of results. For example, hit 10 serves out of a ball hopper and tell yourself that you have to make at least 8, 9, or 10 out of 10 in the box or else there is a penalty. Remember, you will only be able to simulate nerves in this drill setting if the penalty is real and if, on some level, it is something that you fear. It could be a physical penalty, like running sprints. If that doesn't create tension, figure out something that does make you nervous. No cell phone for the rest of the day, no coffee the next morning, etc. My advice to you is to be creative. The possibilities are endless.

Chapter 10

Play Within the Gray

Tennis is not a perfectionist's sport. Have you ever heard of a golden set? This happens when a singles player or doubles team wins an entire set without losing a single point. This certainly doesn't happen very often. When it does, it is usually because one player/team is far more advanced than the other. Honestly, I have never even heard of a golden match, although it might have been done before.

You must accept the fact that you are going to lose points, games, sets, and even matches. You might hit some amazing shots, but still lose the point. I have played countless points in matches where I hit a terrible shot only to see my opponent miss the next one. My reaction inevitably was "I got away with that one." You must be willing to accept this reality before the match begins. But, what are your acceptable levels of tolerance? This is the gray area that you must navigate through in order to play your best on that day and give yourself the best chance to win…on that day.

There are so many variables that can influence a tennis match, which makes seeking perfection virtually impossible. Sun, wind, the type of court, you and/or your partner's energy level, mood, etc. These aren't meant to be excuses for poor play, rather the gray area that must be considered before stepping onto the court. Be able to define what is and is not acceptable in terms of your own quality of play. As a result, you will be able to maintain emotional control thereby giving you the best chance to play your best.

In my experience, there are two primary types of tennis perfectionists that tend to be most prevalent. These perfectionists have varying degrees of severity:

1. *Result-oriented perfectionist:* This player either won the point or lost the point…period. Success if they won the point, failure if they lost the point. It really makes no difference how the result happened, it just did. They would love to hit clean strokes and be positioned correctly. But deep down, they are perfectly fine with doing everything wrong as long as they win the point. You should know by now that this player needs to start focusing on process-oriented thoughts if they really want to play their best. But, playing their best

is not even on their radar in matches because all they care about is winning. This player struggles mightily with logical/process thinking and retreats very quickly to comfort zones. As a result, game improvement for this player can be extremely slow or non-existent.

2. *Stroke-oriented perfectionist:* This is a very dangerous perfectionist that I have seen at many levels. This player is forever seeking the perfect forehand, serve, backhand, volley, or overall game. This is what I call a "feel good" player and their happiness comes from striking the perfect ball. They really want to win, and hitting good strokes is their way to get there. This is the player who can look really good, but still lose to seemingly lesser players because of their fixation on "feeling it." Don't get me wrong, if your strokes aren't up to par, your game will definitely suffer. But, I guarantee that no player in history has ever played a golden set in terms of stroke perfection. It's a losing cause because there will always be strokes that weren't quite good enough, even if the player played well overall and won the match. This mindset is so dangerous because if consumed with feeling the perfect stroke, the player is unable to see the big picture within a tennis match. This causes them to end up out of position, make unforced errors with their other strokes, hit to the wrong targets, and generally have no idea what strategy works against a particular opponent. The bottom line for this player is that a lost point simply means that they have to feel better with that stroke(s).

If you can relate to either of these perfectionists on some level and you want to improve, make sure you have a process "trigger" for your stroke(s). Your trigger should be the one technical thought you have as you are about to hit the ball, which gives you the best chance to execute it well. I would advise you to take a lesson from a certified teaching pro who can help you determine your triggers. I like to think of triggers as the glue that holds the stroke together. Again, it doesn't mean that the entire stroke will be perfect. Your trigger simply gives you the best chance to execute the stroke well. If you correctly execute that trigger, you need to accept the result and continue on, even if you miss the shot. If you did miss the shot while correctly executing your trigger, you should view the error as an acceptable miss. This will keep you in emotional control and help you see the big picture regarding the match you are currently playing. If you find that you miss backhand after backhand throughout a match, then you will need stroke work after the match to improve your backhand and reevaluate your trigger.

Keep in mind that your triggers may shift over the course of time from one technical focal point to another as you continue to play matches and practice. But, save that stroke work for after the match. If you fixate on strokes during the match, you will struggle to manage the match strategically and lose sight of how to maximize the rest of your game.

Within a match, your stroke triggers should only be first on the priority list just before you strike the ball and for a few correctional seconds after you make an unforced error…that's it. The rest of your thinking should be devoted to formations/positioning, team chemistry, and strategy. It might seem backwards that accepting lower-quality strokes will help you win. But the truth is that you only have so much mental energy. If all of that energy is going to your strokes, you will come off the court with no real idea why you won or lost. Remember the priority list from Section 1: Positioning first, then targets, and strokes come last.

To you overachievers, it may sound like I am telling you to lower your expectations. In truth, I am just asking you to make them realistic. But on a deeper level, I am asking you to identify those specific expectations that are difficult to meet and then define your acceptable levels of tolerance. There is no sense in playing a tennis match where you are mentally set up to fail before the first point is played. As stated earlier, when you do fail to meet a high expectation, your emotions will be challenged. And, it's all downhill from there.

Side Note: I was once asked in a lesson how many double faults are acceptable for a whole match. I replied, "You are allowed to double fault as many times as you want as long as you hold serve." This was a result-oriented player that was very troubled by double faults, and I was trying to get my point across. It is good to have goals and expectations for your game, but you must also develop tolerance levels so you stay level headed and give your entire game the best chance to succeed on that day.

Chapter 11

Play to the Score

For most of my playing days, I would hear various teaching pros and coaches say to forget about the score and play one point at a time. It took me a long time to learn what that truly meant. To play one point at a time does not mean that you literally forget about the score, that's obvious. It simply means that you are emotionally centered and aren't allowing the score to influence how well you play. How do you feel when you are down 6-0, 5-0 in a match? Up a set and 5-4 in the second set against a player you have never beaten? Tied at 8-8 in the third set tie-breaker? Many of you can probably relate to each of these scores and recall specific opponents that were involved. You can probably also recall how you felt in each of those moments.

We can't control the initial feeling that hits us in various moments on the tennis court, but we can control how we respond to those feelings, as discussed earlier by focusing on the process. In doing so, we can also be sure that those feelings don't influence our decision making. I am sure you have seen matches where early on all four players are ripping serves and returns, closing the net and firmly striking their volleys, etc. But, watch that same match in the third set tie-breaker and those same players are softly blooping the ball back and forth. These players are afraid to lose and are certainly being influenced by the score. Try your best to maintain emotional control, focus on your process, and you will find yourself successfully playing one point at a time.

You win some, you lose some…just make sure you win the right ones

Years ago, all tennis matches were played by using a two-out-of-three full set scoring format. I remember just how important it was to win that first set, especially if it was a long, close set. The idea of having to win two sets in a row after playing a long, grueling first set in a losing effort was a mentally daunting task. But, with the 10-point tie-breaker replacing the third full set in most tournament and league matches, it is far less important to win the first set.

In my opinion, the most important games of a match today are the first three games of the second set. If you won the first, you are off and rolling in the second set and seemingly on your way to a straight set win. If you lost the first set, getting off to a good start in the second set means you should be headed to a 10-point tie-breaker, which makes the match up for grabs. In addition, winning the second set means you should have some momentum going into the tie-breaker. If someone gave me a choice to win the first or the second set before going into a 10-point tie-breaker, I would definitely choose the second set, so I could have momentum leading into the tie-breaker. Treat the first set as a momentum builder leading into the second set. If you and your partner come out on fire in the first set, make sure you stick with your team strategy and try to sustain your good play (through process-oriented thoughts!) as long as possible. Conversely, you might start a match flat while your opponents are playing awesome and end up down 5-0 or 5-1. At this point, don't bag the first set. Accept the fact that you will probably lose that set. But, use the remaining points to improve your play, make a strategic adjustment, and capture some momentum. If you can lose the set 6-3 or better, you probably will start the second set with some momentum on your side. You may even surprise yourself and recover back to 5-5. Even if you lose the set 6-0 or 6-1, try to use every available point in the first set to positively set the tone for the second set. The bottom line is that no matter what happens in the first set, your team should try to reset and come out ready to execute immediately in the second set.

Also, pay attention to any adjustments made by your opponents when starting the second set, especially if you won the first. Most teams make strategic adjustments at the end of a lost first set. In between sets is also a time when a team can switch positions (deuce court player and ad-court player change positions).

Tie-Breakers

Tie-breakers are such a great part of tennis because they add a sudden death feel to the sport. The problem is that most players tend to treat every point in a tie-breaker as if that point is sudden death. Tie-breakers (especially 10-point tie-breakers) can take a good amount of time to complete, which does allow some breathing room when it comes to losing points. An 11-9 tie-breaker is the same as completing five games at love...that's a lot of tennis. Again, it comes down to acceptable levels of tolerance so you have the emotional stability needed to give yourself a chance to play your best. I am going to outline a mental strategy for you that will hopefully relieve some of the pressure felt in tie-breakers. It is result-oriented by design simply to allow yourself to lose points, so your decisions aren't made emotionally.

After the first point of a tie-breaker is played, I want you to view the rest of the tie-breaker as being four point mini tie-breakers. Two of the points your team serves and two of the points your opponents serve. You have three acceptable outcomes within these mini tie-breakers:

1. *Essential Goal:* You win two points, and your opponent wins two points...stalemate. No one has gained, and no one has lost. Your first priority should be to try your best to win your serve points. But, it really doesn't matter if you win your serve points or return points as long as you win two out of the four points.
2. *Winning Goal:* You win three points, and your opponent wins one.
3. *Icing on the Cake:* You win all four points.

At the end of each four point exchange, you mentally reset and start over. This should be easy to do if you are using the Coman Tie-Breaker format (switch sides after the first point and then after every four points). There will inevitably be times when you don't meet your goal and lose the exchange 1-3 or 0-4. To relieve even more pressure, this is fine as long as it doesn't happen too deep into the tie-breaker.

By executing the Winning Goal of three points won to every one lost, you can mathematically still win a 7-point tie-breaker when down 2-5:

- 2-5 -> 5-6 -> **8-6, 9-7,** or **10-8 win.**

You can also win a 10-point tie-breaker when down 3-8:

- 3-8 -> 6-9 -> 9-10 -> **12-10, 13-11,** or **14-12 win.**

Granted, in order to win from that far behind, you need to win the right three points out of every four (for example, you must win the first three points out of four when down 6-9 or else you lose). But, it should give you hope when you fall behind and feel the tie-breaker slipping away.

Remember, the whole idea here is to help give yourself a way to approach tie-breakers in a way that reduces pressure. Reset at the end of each four point exchange and be willing to implement the best team strategy for that moment. The additional breathing room will help you make logical decisions regarding your strategy and execute better during the point. It should make it easier for you to not panic when you fall behind. Make sure you and your partner work together to stay on task within this system.

Drills for Practice

Get together with three other players and play tie-breakers. Undoubtedly, no one will feel nervous because it is just practice. But, you can start training your mind to reset at the end of each four point exchange. Evaluate how many points out of four you won and make strategic adjustments as necessary. Allow yourself to lose points within this framework in practice so you can take the same thought process to those important matches where you would ordinarily feel nervous on every point.

Chapter 12

Momentum

Tennis is definitely a game of momentum. You can't always control when you have it, but you can do your best to capture and keep it. To do so, you must first be able to identify which team has it. That's not always as easy as it may seem. Sometimes the score makes it obvious. Whether the score is one-sided or close, know which team has the momentum and then do your best to either keep it on your side or steal it from your opponent. Earlier, I briefly covered momentum and how it relates to the 2-out-of-3 set with a 10-point tie-breaker scoring format. In addition, there is a very basic way to determine which team has the overall momentum in a match, and it might surprise you how well it applies to all levels of play.

The basis upon which I like to define who has momentum is by determining which team is holding serve the easiest. Understandably, holding your serve is more important at higher levels of play because the serve quality increases as the level of play increases (speed, spin, accuracy), which makes it more difficult to break serve. However, I would argue that at all levels if you can hold your serve quickly, you have a good chance to gain momentum. If you play at a 3.0 level, you might not hit a high percentage of aces. But, you can try to hold your serve quickly by using all of the other shots and strategies described in Section 1. Let's look at a couple of examples to illustrate what I mean:

- Team A is holding serve easily (at love or 15 each game). Plus, they are also breaking serve every other game...3-1 (5-2 or 6-1. Obvious, right? Any spectator can see from the score that the winning team has momentum.

- Team A is holding serve easily at love or 15 in roughly 2-3 minutes. Team B is also holding serve, but Team B is fighting off break points and playing multiple deuce points. Team B is winning their service games in roughly 8-10 minutes. At 3-3 in the first set, the average spectator might not see which team has the momentum. But, the difficulty Team B is having holding their serve indicates that the momentum is with Team A.

- Team A is holding serve easily and Team B is holding serve easily. Momentum is not yet with either team. Whoever can first extend the length of a return game will start to gain momentum.

- Both Team A and Team B are exchanging holds and breaks of serve while playing out long games. The score remains very close. Again, essentially a stalemate. If either team can hold serve quickly, they will begin to capture the momentum.

The common denominator here is that each scenario involves getting in and out of your service games as quickly as possible. In addition, you are also doing everything you can to extend the length of your return games and potentially break serve.

I am not suggesting that you play quickly in between points on your serve and slowly when returning. You must play at a speed in between points that allows you to play your best. Some like to play quickly while some play slower. What I want you to understand is that when up 40-0 on your serve, put as much focus and energy into winning that point as you would if you were down break point. Conversely, when down 40-0 in a return game, do your best to scrap out as many points as possible to extend the game. You may not win that return game, but you may pull a little more momentum your way leading into your next service game. Plus, you may just surprise yourself and squeak out a service break.

SECTION 2

FINAL THOUGHTS

I view Section 2 as the section of intangibles. The topics discussed are a collection of little things that can make a significant difference in a match. It's possible that you already apply some of the topics, but never really thought of what you were doing because it just came naturally. Whether these ideas are completely new to you or I simply articulated what it is that you already intuitively do in matches, I hope this section helps to give you some concrete methods regarding how to get the most out of your game as well as your partner's. Every player has their own unique set of quirks and personality traits and it is important to mesh yours with your partner's to play the best team doubles possible. Use the guidelines in this section to help you play your best on any given day, and you will be much happier with the results, whether you won or lost.

Similar to Section 1, you will need to practice in order to improve. Most of the topics discussed in this section require that your practice time involves point play. While it is helpful to play practice matches in a safe environment (emphasis on improvement rather than winning), the real test is to apply these topics to those matches that you really want to win. Don't beat yourself up if you are unsuccessful, just pinpoint where you fell short and adjust next time. Improvement is sometimes hard to see, so take the topics and try to focus on one or two at a time. The better you get at executing these intangibles, the more consistent you will play.

Conclusion

If you have studied this book all the way through, you clearly want to improve as a doubles player. There are many tennis players who continue to hit the same shots to the same targets while standing in the same place on the court. They interact with their partner(s) the same way day in and day out. They win some, they lose some. For these people, this is all they need from their tennis to make them happy and there is absolutely nothing wrong with that. But, you want more. You want to know how to improve and the idea of focusing on team positioning and the intangibles in between points makes you want to find a court and get to work.

As for your progress, make sure you are patient. Be sure that you have a clear purpose when you go out to play. In addition, continue to evaluate by asking the important questions. For example:

1. What am I getting better at today?
2. What are my comfort zones and am I willing to be uncomfortable to get better?
3. When I work on stroke mechanics, is it because I can't execute a particular team formation and I need stroke improvement to get better within that formation?
4. Do I help my partner play better or make them play worse?
5. Do I want to make strategic team decisions based primarily on how I like to play? Am I willing to do what makes the most strategic sense, regardless of my own comfort zones?
6. How do I handle nerves?

These are some tough questions to ask and should be done on an ongoing basis. My advice to you when asking these questions is to be honest. You will improve only if you can honestly self-evaluate. You might even need to ask a good tennis friend or your doubles partner for their opinion. Stress to them that you want the truth, nothing sugar-coated. Their point of view might give you some new insight into your game.

Lastly, as you continue to implement and improve on the topics in this book, take time to look back on how you were playing six months ago, one year ago, five years ago, etc. Because improvement can sometimes be very slow, it can feel like you're not getting any better in some or many areas. It can be very easy to lose sight of your own improvement. But over time, you might unknowingly become the savvy doubles veteran that you always admired when looking at other seasoned players. And when you do recognize your own improvement, take time to pause and be proud of yourself for stretching your limits and doing what many players are not willing to do. Recognize your own "I did it" moments and use them to fuel your continued desire to get better. When applying Section 1, you and your partner should enjoy some real "We did it" moments, which is the triumphant teamwork experience doubles can provide, regardless of your playing level. The icing on the cake is that this continued improvement will result in better team play and more wins.

About the Author-Derek Myers

Derek has over 30 years of experience on the tennis court, both as a player and a teacher.

As a player, he was the Indiana High School State Singles Champion, was ranked as high as #8 nationally in USTA junior doubles, and was the recipient of the Bill Talbert National Junior Sportsmanship Award in 1995. While playing at Purdue University, he was a 2-time team MVP, 3-time co-captain, and an All-Big Ten Conference Player. He has the record for most doubles wins in school history and was ranked as high as #7 in the country in the NCAA Division I Men's Doubles rankings. Professionally, he accumulated 13 ATP doubles points in Professional Futures and Challenger events. Most recently in 2013, he and his team won the USTA League National Championship at the 5.0+ 18-and-over level.

Derek has also taught tennis at every level. While pursuing his Master's Degree at Purdue, he was the Assistant Men's Tennis Coach where he was named Assistant Coach of the Year for the NCAA's Region IV in 2002. He has coached numerous junior players who developed into nationally ranked juniors as well as college players. In addition, he has worked extensively with adult players ranging from NTRP levels 3.0-4.5. He is currently the Head Tennis Professional at Roanoke Country Club in Roanoke, VA and is USPTA Certified as an Elite Professional.

Printed in Great Britain
by Amazon